Twayne's Filmmakers Series

Warren French
EDITOR

Howard Hawks

Howard Hawks on location filming El Dorado *(1967).*

Howard Hawks

LELAND A. POAGUE

Iowa State University

BOSTON

Twayne Publishers

1982

Howard Hawks

is published in 1982 by Twayne Publishers,
A Division of G. K. Hall & Co.

Copyright © 1982 by G. K. Hall & Co.

Printed on permanent/durable acid-free paper
and bound in the United States of America

First Printing, July 1982

Production Stills courtesy of the Museum of
Modern Art/Film Stills Archive.

Library of Congress Cataloging in Publication Data

Poague, Leland A., 1948–
Howard Hawks.

(Twayne's filmmakers series)
Bibliography: p. 165–172
Filmography: p. 173–192
Includes index.
1. Hawks, Howard, 1896–1977.
I. Title.   II. Series.
PN1998.A3H353   791.43′0233′0924   82-961
ISBN 0-8057-9285-6   AACR2

Contents

About the Author

Leland Poague holds degrees from San Jose State College and the University of Oregon, has taught literature and film criticism in the SUNY system and at the University of Rochester, and is presently an associate professor of English at Iowa State University. He has written books on Frank Capra (1975) and Ernst Lubitsch (1978). His most recent book is *The Hollywood Professionals Vol. 7: Wilder & McCarey* (1980). He is also coauthor with William Cadbury of *Film Criticism: A Counter Theory*, forthcoming from the Iowa State University Press. Dr. Poague is a frequent contributor to film journals, *Film Criticism, Movietone News,* and *Literature/Film Quarterly* among them. Much of his research for the present book was undertaken while participating in a National Endowment for the Humanities seminar on "The Classical Narrative Cinema and Modernist Alternatives" directed by Professor David Bordwell at the University of Wisconsin–Madison.

Editor's Foreword

Some understandable reservations have been expressed that the rather rigid format of this series might oblige authors, lacking adequate space for significant original comment, to resort to clichéd judgments. We hope it will be remembered, however, that many contributions to our series are the first book-length studies of visionary directors like Anthony Mann, Sam Peckinpah, and Douglas Sirk, for example, while others—like the books on Fritz Lang and Pasolini—are the first addressed to American undergraduates rather than sophisticated film scholars. The authors have, therefore, faced the problem of both acquainting new audiences with the directors themselves and charting the contours of their careers, as well as estimating their significance.

That the series provides also an opportunity for fresh depth studies was demonstrated early by Annette Insdorf's *François Truffaut*, in which this well-known and much discussed director's career is not just once more reviewed, but in which, rather, certain of his most important films are studied at length to demonstrate the importance of conspicuous influences and tendencies in his work.

Such a book is the present one on Howard Hawks. Certainly another introduction to Hawks is not required. He has already been the subject of well-circulated books by Peter Bogdanovich (1962), Robin Wood (1968), John Belton (1974), and Donald Willis (1975), as well as Peter Wollen's influential *Signs and Meaning in the Cinema* (1969, revised 1972), which synthesizes earlier studies, including the essays by such respected figures as French "New Wave" director/critic Jacques Rivette.

Poague's principal point is indeed that most of this abundant and intensive criticism has been wrong-headed, especially in promoting the now clichéd image of Hawks as a kind of embittered "waste land" Modernist, cynically portraying mankind as the tragic victim of a

hostile universe. Poague "reads" Hawks's most characteristic films in
a quite different way, so that his purpose is not to reinforce but
challenge the prevailing view.

This effort has required a considerable departure from the general
format of this series. Since Hawks came from an affluent background
and spent his Hollywood years developing professionally and avoid-
ing the kind of bizarre behavior that made many other movie people
newsworthy, interest resides not in the man but his work. Since also
Poague seeks to replace complex concepts of this work with his own
even subtler theories, long and meticulously detailed studies of a few
key works are required rather than summary reviews of films that
have already been the subject of hundreds of "notes" at Film Society
showings.

It would be improper here to preempt Poague's own patient,
inductive development of his countertheses about Hawks; but
readers who come to the book with certain kinds of preconceptions (of
the very nature that Poague finds at the root of many of Hawks's
characters' problems) may need to be prepared for its nonchronologi-
cal structure.

Poague begins with two familiar films representative of Hawks's
"adventures" and "comedies"—*Only Angels Have Wings* (1939) and
I Was a Male War Bride (1949)—to announce his theories that are at
odds with familiar interpretations of the vision informing these films.
He then flashes back to the silent era to examine certain early Hawks
films that he feels have been insufficiently closely scrutinized in order
to show how they may serve "as a general introduction to certain
characteristic thematic and stylistic features of the Hawksian
cinema."

The fourth chapter then views many of Hawks's darkest "adventure" films of the 1930s, like *Scarface,* not as existential visions of
man's helpless place in an absurd universe, but rather as essentially
transcendentalist revelations of the destructive inflexibility of human
social codes. This downbeat account provides, however, the background for a final reconsideration of the post–World War II *Red River*
as an upbeat reworking of this model of the Depression years. In the
fifth chapter, Poague shuttles rapidly back and forth across Hawks's
career from early silent films like *Fig Leaves* to *Man's Favorite Sport?*
(1964) to challenge the commonplace assumption that the women in
Hawks's films function as threats to group unity and masculinity itself
and to substitute for it a concept of Hawks as a classic exponent of the

American film's emphasis on the importance of heterosexual relationships.

Poague's final chapter comprises a set of notes for an extended reading of *Rio Bravo* that might itself be as long as this whole book. In these he softspokenly stands on its head the received opinion that this "most obligatory" of Hawks's films for the aspiring critic has the whole tradition of the Hawks canon and the Western genre behind it. As this summary suggests, this is a book that seeks not to close discussion of Hawks and consign him to the museum, but to open it.

I would like to begin the response myself by posing one question that Poague properly does not touch upon in his effort to document his case for a reinterpretation of Hawks's work—the more impressionistic one of why, if Poague's speculations are valid, Hawks's films have been so consistently misread?

On the final page of this study, Lee Poague pays tribute to Hawks's continued celebration in his films of the values of "wit, intelligence, and sexuality." In completely rethinking the films he is obliged to concentrate largely on their sexual implications; but their other two qualities merit equally extended study, especially in this "witless" age.

Understandably, modern film criticism has downplayed the "talking" aspect of "talking pictures" in order to stress a still printbound public's imperceptions of the nature of the visual experience. Partly as a result of the recent concentration on *looking at* movies, the dialogue in recent films—what there is of it—is rarely worth listening to. One recalls the brilliance of the dialogue in films like Hawks's *Bringing Up Baby* in contrast to, for example, the characters' reflection of the creator's fatal inarticulateness in Michael Cimino's *Heaven's Gate*.

I suspect that a great problem in interpreting Hawks's films is that audiences have not listened to what is being said, but have instead supplied the dialogue that fits their own preconceptions of the situations projected before them (always a particular danger in a poor speaker like John Wayne's association with a stereotyped point of view). What arrests attention in the book that follows is Poague's unemphasized pointing out of the way that Hawks's ultimately affirmative narratives have generally been misinterpreted in terms of the fashionable "Decline of the West" philosophies of the 1920s and 1930s and the existential despair of the years after World War II. We have needed a good listener like Lee Poague to argue with reference to chapter and verse that Hawks did not speak *for* the popular mind of his time, but *to* it, although its ear missed his nuances as it does most transcendental messages. If this observation is valid, we have only begun to deal adequately with the work of a truly *classic* artist.

W. F.

Preface

This is a critical study of the films of Howard Hawks. My immediate goal in writing it has been to discern and describe those significantly recurrent features of style—i.e., of theme, structure, character, and image—which may be said to constitute the "Hawksian cinema." My thesis, to the extent that I have a single thesis, is that the Hawksian cinema is even more unified, coherent, and intensely expressive than has hitherto been demonstrated. Indeed, as I hope to show in my second chapter, I believe that much serious and admirable Hawks criticism has erected, by what I take to be errors of emphasis and omission, something of a barrier to a fuller appreciation of the aesthetic experience which those films may be said to offer us.

Implicit in the specific critical purpose outlined above is a larger end-in-view, to borrow a phrase from Monroe Beardsley.[1] I assume that *aesthetic experience* of the sort made possible by the films of Howard Hawks is inherently valuable, both to human beings as individuals and to human cultures and societies in general; and I assume as well the corollary—that the value of a particular *aesthetic object* is a function of its ability to invite and sustain our attention, whether or not we agree in retrospect with the values embodied by the object. Put another way, I am not concerned here with sociology—with how the films of Howard Hawks *have* functioned. I am concerned, rather, with how they *might* function, for myself and for others who are willing to attend to them.

The question then becomes: why attend to objects which we do not believe or with which we do not agree? And C. S. Lewis provides an answer: because "we seek an enlargement of our being."[2] This is true in at least two respects. First, to read a novel or play or to see a film is to undergo an experience unavailable except through that novel, play, or film. Other experiences may be like it, and one can insist on ethical grounds that certain such experiences are preferable to others, but any such experience is unique in its totality and

11

specificity, however much certain of its elements may recall and resonate to elements in other works. More important, however, is the fact that aesthetic objects allow us to expand our experience of values. This is particularly true of narrative arts where the values celebrated in any given work are clearly human values, having to do with attitudes and actions and points of view.[3] Only in instances where a work exhaustively replicates our own life-values will the work be valueless from this perspective.

The primary function of criticism, under such a theory, is therefore to describe the values at play in the works of its subject. Value judgments, by this logic, are only of secondary interest. Indeed, value judgments as typically pronounced tend as often to cut off description and attention as promote them. To say that "Hawks isn't good enough" is ultimately to imply that we should not view his films.[4] But once we have expressed a willingness to attend to the films, the question is reversed: are *we* good enough? Can we take full advantage of the film experience by letting the texts be distinctively themselves? In order to encourage an appreciative awareness of the Hawksian cinema it is therefore necessary to describe my under-standing of the films and how they work, both generally, as a group, and individually, through the analysis of representative films. Such is my primary task for the remainder of this book.

LELAND POAGUE

Iowa State University

Acknowledgments

My thanks are due first to the administration and faculty of Iowa State University—for giving me the opportunity to complete my writing and research. Especial thanks to Vice President Daniel Zaffarano, to Dean Wallace Russell, and to Professors Frank Haggard, Donald Benson, and Gretchen Bataille—all were instrumental in providing me with research support and release time. I am grateful to Robert Carringer, Richard Ramsey, Richard Gollin, and Warren French for encouraging me to undertake the project. Screenings were arranged with the kind assistance of James Card and Marshall Deutelbaum of the George Eastman House; Emily Sieger, Barbara Humphrys, and the staff of the Motion Picture Section of the Library of Congress; Charles Silver of the Museum of Modern Art/Film Study Center; Susan Dalton and Maxine Fleckner of the Wisconsin Center for Film and Theatre Research; Allen Estrin of Films Incorporated; and Rachel Opheim of the Iowa State University Media Resources Center. I profited from the editorial advice of David Tedlock, Marshall Deutelbaum, Gary Hooper, Charles L. P. Silet, and Terri Paul—to all of whom I offer my sincere thanks. Stills were provided, in part, by the Museum of Modern Art/Film Stills Archive; thanks to Mary Corliss. Special debts are owed to William Cadbury, with whom I first studied Hawks and whose influence is particularly noteworthy in my discussions of *Road to Glory* and *Red River*, and also to Robin Wood, whose book on Hawks continues to be a model of critical practice—however much I have come to disagree with certain of his positions. Professor Wood was kind enough to provide me with a draft version of the introduction to the second edition of his Hawks monograph; my chapter 5 is particularly indebted to this material. Of the many students who have influenced my thinking on Hawks Cindy Skeates stands out; in thanking her I thank them all. Thanks are also due Sheryl Kamps, Jane Seddigh, Sue Gordon, Tina Compton, and Carol Lamb—together they worked miracles in typing the manuscript. Much of the work of compiling the filmography was done by Catherine Pierson—to whom I am very grateful. I am also grateful to my wife, Susan Poague, for her ongoing patience and support, and to Rudy and Sylvia Rucker and Jim and Jo-Ann Skinner for their friendship and support. For better than a decade now Jon and Carol Sanford have done their utmost to encourage my work; their hospitality over the years has made it possible for me to do the research upon which my scholarship necessarily depends. To Jon and Carol, then, I dedicate this book—and to their daughter, Susan Sanford.

Chronology

1896	Howard Winchester Hawks born May 30, Goshen, Indiana, to Frank and Helen Hawks. (Their two other sons, Kenneth and William, would also become involved with motion pictures.)
1908	The Hawks family moves to Pasadena, California.
1914	Attends Philips-Exeter Academy.
1916	Works in the property department of the Famous Players–Lasky (later Paramount) Studio during his summer vacation from college.
1917	Graduates with degree in engineering from Cornell University; returns to Famous Players–Lasky, where he directs scenes for Marshall Neilan's *The Little Princess*.
1918– 1922	Serves during World War I as an Army Air Corps flight instructor, stationed in Texas; thereafter works building and flying airplanes and driving racing cars.
1922– 1924	Independently produces two-reel comedies for such directors as Marshall Neilan, Allan Dwan, and Allen Holubar; works on production, scripts, and casting for Paramount and MGM. Scenarios and stories from this period include those for Jack Conway's *Quicksands* (1923; rereleased 1927), George Melford's *Tiger Love* (1924), Paul Bern's *The Dressmaker from Paris* (released 1925), and Josef Von Sternberg's *Underworld* (released 1926; original conception and scenario by Hawks and Ben Hecht).
1925	Moves to Fox.
1926	Directs first feature films, *The Road to Glory* and *Fig Leaves*; does scriptwork on Chester Bennett's *Honesty—The Best Policy*.
1927	Directs *The Cradle Snatchers* and *Paid to Love*.
1928	*A Girl in Every Port, Fazil, The Air Circus*.
1929	*Trent's Last Case*.

1930   Directs his first talking film, *The Dawn Patrol*; the story, credited to John Monk Saunders but ghost written by Hawks, receives academy award. *Scarface* is filmed but withheld from distribution until 1932.

1931   *The Criminal Code.*

1932   *The Crowd Roars, Tiger Shark*, scriptwork on Victor Fleming's *Red Dust.*

1933   *Today We Live*; is replaced as director of *The Prizefighter and the Lady* by W. S. Van Dyke.

1934   Scripts *Viva Villa!* with Ben Hecht; shoots location footage in Mexico; but is replaced as director by Jack Conway. Directs *Twentieth Century.*

1935   *Barbary Coast, Ceiling Zero.*

1936   *The Road to Glory, Come and Get It*; scriptwork on James Cruz's *Sutter's Gold.*

1937   Scriptwork on Victor Fleming's *Captains Courageous.*

1938   *Bringing Up Baby*; does scriptwork on Victor Fleming's *Test Pilot; The Dawn Patrol* is remade by Edmund Goulding.

1939   *Only Angels Have Wings*; does scriptwork on Victor Fleming's *Gone With the Wind* and George Stevens's *Gunga Din*; Lloyd Bacon remakes *The Crowd Roars* as *Indianapolis Speedway.*

1940   *His Girl Friday*; scripts *The Outlaw* with Jules Furthman and completes ten days of shooting before producer Howard Hughes takes over direction himself.

1941   *Sergeant York, Ball of Fire.*

1943   *Air Force*; produces Richard Rosson's *Corvette K-225.*

1944   *To Have and Have Not.*

1946   *The Big Sleep.*

1948   *Red River, A Song Is Born.*

1949   *I Was a Male War Bride.*

1951   Produces *The Thing*, directed by Christian Nyby.

1952   *The Big Sky*; "The Ransom of Red Chief" episode of the omnibus film *O. Henry's Full House*; *Monkey Business.*

1953   *Gentlemen Prefer Blondes.*

1955   *Land of the Pharaohs.*

1959   *Rio Bravo.*

1962   *Hatari!*

1963   *Man's Favorite Sport?*

1965   *Red Line 7000.*

1967   *El Dorado.*
1970   *Rio Lobo.*
1977   Hawks dies, December 26, in Palm Springs, California.

1

Hawks and the Critics

THE MOST GENERALLY ACCEPTED VIEW of the cinema of Howard Hawks, certainly among Anglo-American critics, is that put forth by Peter Wollen in *Signs and Meaning in the Cinema*. Partly this results from the fact that Wollen's chapter on the auteur theory, wherein Hawks and Ford provide the primary data, was one of the key texts in the ascendancy of auteurism as a director-centered philosophy of film criticism in the late 1960s; Wollen's chapter is still frequently reprinted in textbook anthologies.[1] There is also the fact that Wollen's discussion of semiology (particularly in the 1972 revision of the book) was central to the subsequent and rapid rise of that school of film criticism in its turn. Wollen's book has thus been a crucial text in the development of film theory for over a decade now—so that people with a limited knowledge of Hawks are likely to have derived their general view of his films almost exclusively from Wollen's description of the Hawksian cinema: it's the Wollen view of Hawks which dominates, both in the criticism and in general histories and casual references.[2]

To single out Wollen for scrutiny and rebuttal is not to imply that Wollen was any sort of maverick, no more so than most Hawks critics. To be accurate, it must be said that Wollen's view of Hawks is very deeply indebted to the work of previous critics, particularly Jacques Rivette, Andrew Sarris, Peter Bogdanovich, and Robin Wood. But most of this scholarship was not generally or easily available during the crucial period (1969–1972) wherein Wollen's view of Hawks gained ascendancy. Much of this pre-Wollen work, however, has since been reprinted, in Joseph McBride's *Focus on Howard Hawks* anthology, and it will help to clarify Wollen's argument if we briefly fill in the critical context wherein it developed.[3]

Hawks consults with Humphrey Bogart and Lauren Bacall during the filming of The Big Sleep *(1946).*

During most of his creative lifetime Hawks was largely ignored by the critical establishment, particularly in America. To the French critics of Truffaut's generation must therefore go the honor of "discovering" Hawks. His films were regularly reviewed in French periodicals and film journals from the early 1950s onward; Jacques Rivette's ground-breaking essay "Génie de Howard Hawks" appeared in *Cahiers du Cinéma* in 1953 (Truffaut's famous article on the auteur theory appeared in 1954), and the Rivette piece was followed in 1956 by the publication in *Cahiers* of an extended interview with Hawks conducted by Truffaut, Rivette, and Jacques Becker.[4]

The real breakthrough in Hawks criticism, however, occurred in 1962 and early 1963. During the summer of 1962 Peter Bogdanovich organized a Hawks retrospective for the Museum of Modern Art, in connection with which he prepared a monograph on Hawks consisting of an introductory essay and a long interview cum filmography. At the same time Andrew Sarris was (evidently) at work on his long overview article on Hawks, which first appeared in the *New York Film Bulletin* in 1961 and which was subsequently expanded for publication in two parts in the July and August numbers of the British film journal *Films and Filming*. In December 1962 another British journal, *Movie*, published a special Hawks issue, containing articles by several critics, Robin Wood, V. F. Perkins, and Mark Shivas among them; but also included were an abbreviated version of the Bogdanovich monograph (which, in January 1963, was reprinted yet again in a special Hawks issue of *Cahiers* [No. 139]) and an edited version of Rivette's original Hawks essay.[5] The essays collected in *Movie* 5 were hardly monolithic in their approach to Hawks—indeed, the pieces by V. F. Perkins are interesting precisely for their independence—but by and large the essays were printed around and written in response to the Bogdanovich and Rivette contributions (both are frequently cited in the other articles) and it was the Rivette/Bogdanovich view of Hawks which dominated.

Several critical emphases are recurrent in the Hawks scholarship which came out of the early 1960s. It is repeatedly observed, for example, that Hawks's films are "divided equally between comedy and drama" (Rivette, 19)—and while the frequent admixture of the two in particular films is often noted (Bogdanovich says that the genres are "interchangeable" [5]), the tendency is to describe Hawks's adventure films and comedies as moving in opposite directions. As Andrew Sarris put it: "Hawks approached his adventures affirmatively and his comedies negatively" (61). Despite the differences in pace and treatment, however, it is generally agreed that at base Hawks's dramas and comedies evidence the same bitterly tragic vision of the cosmos (see Bogdanovich, 5, Rivette, 19, and Sarris, 35). Tragedy in the adventure films, or so it is argued, finds expression through the metaphor of male professionalism—"the heroism and presumption of men in impossible situations" (Sarris, 38). As Bogdanovich puts it: "His men are gallant but their deaths are inevitable; theirs is a happy-go-lucky recklessness that is really the facade for a fatalistic approach to a world in which they hold a very tenuous position" (5). The universe of the adventure films is thus a universe of war, crime, brutality, and violence—all of which are manifestations of "The unnatural order with which man must cope" (Sarris, 51). Even women in the adventure films, at least as Sarris describes them, represent the general hostility of the cosmos. They are, he says in reference to *Tiger Shark* (1932), "an inexorable force of nature which mercilessly rejects the physically imperfect" (41).

A tragic vision is also at the heart of Hawksian comedy according to the early critics. If anything, "Hawksian comedy is even more bitter than Hawksian adventure" (Sarris, 43). In the adventure films, at least, it is possible for Hawks's heroes to leave society behind and confront death directly—on the frontier, on the race course, in the sky, in South America or Africa or at the North Pole, etc. But, as Peter Bogdanovich first noted, Hawksian comedy generally takes place *within* society, exploiting its "insanities" (5) for satiric effect. Hence the central paradox in the comedies: civilization is generally (or so this line of argument goes) far from civilized. Indeed, as Rivette has it, the central impulse in the comedies is "the allure of natural instincts, the surrender to earthly, primitive forces, evil, ugliness, stupidity" (19). Thus it's "the inhuman excesses of the modern world" (Sarris, 49) that Hawks attacks in the comedies, "the regression of man to a lower order" (Sarris, 47). And the chief agent of regression, or so Sarris, at least, implies, is generally the madcap Hawksian female (he mentions Hepburn in *Bringing Up Baby* [1938] and Stanwyck in *Ball of Fire* [1941]).

The degree of Peter Wollen's indebtedness to this general view of Hawks should be self-evident to those familiar with his chapter on the auteur theory. Like Rivette, he begins with the adventure/comedy distinction ("These two types express inverse views of the world, the positive and negative poles of the Hawksian vision" [81])—which he then relates to the themes of heroism and professionalism, both of which are predicated, as Wollen has it, on the assumption that "death

is an absolute limit" which "renders the life which preceded it meaningless, absurd" (81). According to Wollen, Hawks's solution to the
problem of death, a solution embodying a "desolate and barren view
of life" (83), is "the camaraderie of the exclusive, self-sufficient,
all-male group" (82) which, by the imposition of various tests on
newcomers and through the experience of group rituals, "strictly
preserves its exclusivity" (82) against the threats presented by "society" on the one hand and "woman"—often associated with animals
and nature—on the other: society is to be rejected and woman is to be
mastered (88).

Wollen admits that such a worldview is "retrograde" and "stunted"
(90)—but rather than rethink his description of the adventure films
Wollen goes on to propose that Hawks's comedies may in some sense
be said to compensate for this stuntedness by attacking the very
qualities that the adventure films seem to defend. Where the adventure films celebrate an adolescent sort of male ethos, the comedies
expose this adolescence as regression—to childhood, to infantilism,
even to savagery. Where the adventure films celebrate man's mastery
of woman and nature, the comedies demonstrate this mastery to be
an illusion: in the comedies it's the women who wear the pants and
the men who wear the skirts—hence the frequent "scenes of male
humiliation" (91).

We may summarize Wollen's schematic view of Hawks by the
following chart:

		ADVENTURE FILMS	COMEDIES
SOCIETY	CHARAC-TERS	Active characters are primarily or exclusively male: "the group."	Active characters are primarily female: the woman-dominant couple.
	SOCIETY	The larger society is rejected or ignored in favor of an alternative world or an elite society of pro-fessionals.	Society is either the setting for the film's action or it breaks in upon the characters despite their desire for isolation.
CHAOS		Chaos is external and is repre-sented by nature, woman, ani-mals, and death.	Chaos is essentially internal—to society and to individuals—and generally sexual: the expression of female sexuality generally eventuates in regression or sup-pression of the male and his sex-uality.

A final note on the criticism: readers familiar with Robin Wood's more recent work in *Film Comment* will recognize the foregoing chart as an adaptation of Wood's own latter-day view of the adventure/comedy dichotomy in Hawks and of the thematic contrasts and continuities which exist in Hawks across and between the two genres.[6] I have had to adjust the terms of the chart somewhat in order for it to fit Wollen's view of Hawks—but the adjustment has been quite minor. The only real difference is Wood's belief that the outbreak of chaos in the comedies is to be seen positively, as the liberation of socially repressed sexual instincts. That difference aside, Wood's more recent view of Hawks is very much in accord with Wollen's in its broad outlines, despite the fact that Wood, in *Personal Views*, has taken some pains to distance himself from Wollen, at least in terms of methodology.[7]

This similarity of Wood and Wollen is not surprising, however. Indeed, it is clear that Wollen's description of Hawks, while obviously indebted to Rivette et al., is equally indebted to Wood's long out of print 1968 Hawks monograph. Furthermore, it is equally clear that the indebtedness was mutual. Wood acknowledges that Wollen had a particular influence on his own discussion of *El Dorado* (1967); while Wollen cites Wood's discussion of *Scarface* (1930; released 1932), where he groups it with the comedies rather than the adventure films, in order to tie down his own discussion of the regression theme.

If we characterize the changes wrought by Wollen on the Rivette/Bogdanovich/Sarris view of Hawks we find two key shifts of emphasis: Wollen exaggerates the adventure/comedy distinction, making it seem a matter of absolute opposition, and he adds the focus on the Hawksian group, a focus which was largely lacking in the earlier scholarship. Both of these changes can be traced to Wood's book on Hawks. Wood makes the adventure/comedy dichotomy a major factor in the organization of his monograph—and is forced to push the distinction when he argues that *Scarface* ought to be grouped with the comedies. "The overlapping and combining of farce and horror points ahead to *His Girl Friday*, Tony's destructive innocence to that of Lorelei Lee [in *Gentlemen Prefer Blondes*]; in *Monkey Business*, the juxtapositions of ape, savages, and children are clearly related to the presentation of the gangsters in *Scarface*. Above all, *Scarface* gives us the essential theme of Hawks's most characteristic comedies. If the adventure films place high value on the sense of responsibility, the comedies derive much of their tension and intensity from the fascination exerted by irresponsibility" (67–68). And Wood also devoted an entire chapter to "The Group"—though he carefully ob-

serves that "no two Hawks groups are quite the same" (89). Despite
the debts, however, it must be said that Wollen's tendency in para-
phrasing Wood is to exaggerate Wood's points, if only by removing
them from the context provided by Wood's elegantly nuanced discussions of specific films. And it is significant that Wollen ignores
altogether Wood's chapter on "The Instinctive Consciousness"
wherein Wood discusses precisely those qualities in Hawks of flexibility and resiliency which would force Wollen to modify his view that
groups in Hawks are dedicated to a rigid form of elitism. All things
considered, then, it must be said that Wood is far less responsible
than Wollen for the accepted view of Hawks. But it must also be said
that Wood's view of Hawks clearly and generally accords with the
critical tradition which gave rise to Wollen's description of the Hawksian cinema—a description with which I have come increasingly to
disagree as my knowledge of Hawks's films has grown.

2

Countertheory: The Hawksian World View

IN "HAWKS DE-WOLLENIZED" ROBIN WOOD critiques Peter Wollen's description of the films of Howard Hawks in largely methodological terms—and, I must add, with little awareness of the degree to which Wollen's view of Hawks mirrors as well as it distorts Wood's own picture of the Hawksian "metaphysic."[1] Specifically, Wood quite rightly scores Wollen's tendency to ignore specific details (e.g., the expressions and gestures of actors) while attending to abstract structural entities—thematic oppositions, recurrent character alignments, repeated patterns of action, etc. I have argued elsewhere that criticism is precisely a matter of abstraction: it cannot and should not be avoided.[2] The distinction between criticism and more naive modes of perception is that criticism generates and displays its abstractions in a more self-conscious and public manner. But Wood is right to suggest that critical abstractions, if they are to have any validity, must be such that they enrich our knowledge of and hence our response to specific films or texts. That is the ultimate test of any act of criticism. It is a test which the traditional view of Hawks largely fails. Analyzing *Only Angels Have Wings* (1939) and *I Was a Male War Bride* (1949) will help to clarify the nature and degree of that failure and to establish the terms wherein we can offer a tentative countertheory of the Hawksian world view.

Hawksian Adventure: *Only Angels Have Wings* (1939)

The opening moments of *Only Angels Have Wings* are significant in several respects: they set forth certain essential issues and help to establish an iconographic and rhetorical context within which and against which we can read the rest of the film.

Hawks with Jean Arthur during production of Only Angels Have Wings *(1939).*

27

In mimetic terms, the opening sequence (defined here by setting: the dockside) is comprised of three "events": (1) a boat enters a misty South American banana port (Baranca) and ties up; (2) passengers debark while mail sacks are exchanged between armed couriers and a ship's officer; and (3) the couriers follow a woman passenger, who tries to avoid them, but who quickly offers to buy the men a drink when she discovers they are fellow Americans.

The first of these events raises issues both thematic and stylistic. In thematic terms we may understand the event itself as a parable of professional teamwork: hand signals are passed from watch to bridge (we see such signal gestures repeatedly in the film); the ship's horn is sounded; orders are shouted; lines are heaved. But Hawks is not content merely to "describe" the action. Rather, the cutting and camera placement are such that we see the action from a variety of vantage points and distances, as a series of individual acts and as a whole action—and that sense of "wholeness" extends to include setting as well. We see not only a boat docking but we see a good deal of the dockside area as well. And it is precisely this ability to see things in context and from several vantage points that the film is concerned, among other things, to celebrate. Indeed, as Kathleen Murphy points out, "seeing" is one of the film's major themes, both in its action (the mail pilots fly "blind" in the fog; Kid Dabb [Thomas Mitchell] is grounded for poor eyesight) and in its dialogue ("You've got a good eye, lady").[3]

The second event involves the debarkation of passengers and the exchange of mail sacks—but superimposed over the practical or mimetic aspect of the action are matters of language and sexuality. Thus as passengers leave the ship they are told in Spanish that the boat leaves at four o'clock: English-speaking passengers require translation—again, the contrast of vantage point (English) and context (Spanish). Les Peters (Allyn Joslyn) and Joe Souther (Noah Beery, Jr.) then arrive, hand over the mail, and ask Rafael, the ship's officer, "How's the talent this trip?" Context quickly allows us to see that "talent" here is to be understood sexually: despite his disclaimers that there's "not much to choose from," the "pretty mouse" under his right eye (again the sight metaphor) indicates the contrary. Rafael tries to explain that the bruise resulted from rough weather and an unfriendly cabin door knob, but just then Bonnie Lee (Jean Arthur) steps off the boat, says "boo" to Rafael, rocking him back on his heels, and walks off—at which point Les exclaims that she's "the door knob" and Joe declares that they have "some work to do."

The language play connected with the second event of the opening section of *Only Angels Have Wings* thus has the effect of juxtaposing two contexts: sex and work. Both Rafael and then Les and Joe in their turn discuss Bonnie in the language of their profession. For Rafael she is connected with "rough weather" while for Les and Joe she is "talent" with whom they must "work." That juxtaposition—implying a relationship of significant equality or analogy—is further specified by the third event of the opening sequence, Bonnie's attempt to avoid Joe and Les and her subsequent offer to buy the boys a drink.

Again we see the interplay of dramatic action and thematic implication: at one level Les and Joe are simply taking the mail sacks back to Dutchy's bar cum airfield while at another level they are trailing Bonnie as she explores the dockside environs: work and sex go together. And the same is true in some respect for Bonnie. She, too, it turns out, is a "professional," an entertainer in her case, and in seeking to lose Joe and Les she goes to a native cafe where she stands among the doorway crowd to listen to the music and to watch the explicitly sexual movements of the native dancers. Indeed, the sensuality becomes a matter of communal (and cinematic) celebration as Hawks cuts from long full shots into medium and close shots in time with the music, as everyone, Bonnie included, joins in the chorus of the song. This is the first clear indication we get of Bonnie's musical abilities—but the correlation here of self, sexuality, and professionalism is clear enough, and is subtly reinforced, after Joe Souther smashes up his plane and dies, when Bonnie plays the peanut vendor song for and with Jeff Carter (Cary Grant), the man who sent Joe up: several of the musicians from the film's first song sequence appear at Dutchy's, as if to help Bonnie out.

This implicit comparison between the two "singing" scenes in *Only Angels Have Wings* evidences a basic rhetorical strategy (or structural principle) of the film—and of Hawks's films generally—which we may term, alternately, "repetition" or "juxtaposition." Thus the opening sequence of *Only Angels* juxtaposes two sorts of communal activity: the first one primarily "male" in its connotations and images (the boat "enters" the dock; "mail" sacks are delivered by pistol toting guards) and the second primarily female (the ring of spectators, the strummed guitar, the focus on Bonnie in the "entry" way)—though both activities, by their juxtaposition and by their subsequent repetition through the course of the film, are to be read as analogous, and analogously important, activities.

These principles of juxtaposition and repetition are evident at several levels of the text. Thus in structural terms, for example, as Alan Williams has pointed out at length, *Only Angels Have Wings* falls into three sections, differentiated by the alternation of day and night and by the entrance or departure (twice through death) of various characters, but similar to each other in terms of their basic pattern of action.[4] Thus part one begins, as we have seen, with the arrival of Bonnie Lee and her subsequent initiation into the world of the mail pilots; no sooner do Bonnie, Les, and Joe sit down to have a drink than Joe is ordered to fly the mail run. Bad weather forces Joe back and he attempts to land, against Jeff's orders, because he wants to have dinner with Bonnie. The other flyers take Joe's death too much in stride, or so it seems to Bonnie, and she slaps Jeff in her indignation. Jeff sends her outside to cool off. She eventually returns to the bar (the second "singing" scene) and talks with Jeff until he takes off to complete the mail flight that Joe had attempted.

Part two begins in daylight, with Jeff's return and with the arrival, in the next scene, of the next mail shipment and a new pilot, Bat McPherson (Richard Barthelmess), accompanied by his wife, Judy (Rita Hayworth). Bat is then initiated into the group, by flying a dangerous rescue mission; and he is assigned the next mail run, replacing Gent Shelton (John Carrol), who had refused to fly because part of the cargo was nitroglycerin. Again, the flight is aborted due to bad weather, but Bat lands safely after dropping the nitro. He then prepares to resume the flight.

Part three then begins with McPherson's return, at night, after which Judy undergoes an initiation of sorts (Jeff douses her with ice water). The mail arrives and The Kid and McPherson take up the new tri-motor, McPherson having replaced Jeff, who was accidentally shot in the shoulder after Bonnie's attempt to prevent him from taking off in bad weather. The new plane cannot clear the mountains so against Jeff's orders Kid decides to fly "blind" through the weather-shrouded pass. They almost make it but a condor crashes through the windshield (breaking Kid's neck) and other birds (apparently) cause the engines to catch fire. Rather than bail out Bat turns the plane around and crash lands on the field. The Kid dies. At the last minute the weather clears, and Jeff and Les (each man now disabled in one arm) take off to fly the mail run that Kid and Bat had begun—thus fulfilling the air-service contract and earning a government subsidy for future operations. Just before taking off Jeff effectively asks Bonnie not to leave by giving her Kid's two-headed coin.

There are two important aspects or implications of this structural repetition to be remarked upon—both having to do with the relationship among structure, character, and theme. In certain respects, for example, the regularity of life in *Only Angels Have Wings* is a function of place and profession: as a port Baranca is a scene of arrivals and departures, and as flyers Jeff and his crew are repeatedly taking off and landing. But it should be remembered that Jeff Carter is responsible for initiating the air service; he was the one who talked Dutchy into bankrolling the project. And we can reasonably ask why.

The answer is provided, or at least implied, in the character of Bat McPherson. McPherson (aka Kilgallon) ventures to Baranca to escape the past; he had once bailed out of a disabled plane leaving his mechanic to go down with the aircraft (the mechanic, it turns out, was the brother of Kid Dabb—more on this). Likewise, Jeff Carter is a man with a past—though in his case the past is sexual, an unhappy relationship with a woman who couldn't take the fact of his flying, or so Jeff tells the tale to Bonnie. Bat's past and Jeff's past are thus paralleled with one another (both had "bailed out") and the parallelism reinforces the work/sex analogy posited in the film's opening sequence. To be sure, Jeff seems the more courageous of the two, the one least likely to have bailed out for the wrong reasons. But Jeff's sexual courage is clearly called into question through the course of the film. Thus the girl who couldn't take flyers turns out to have married one—Bat McPherson, indeed—which calls Jeff's version of the story somewhat into question. And the problematic nature of Jeff's general attitude toward women is made clear very early in the film.

The ambiguity of Jeff's general sexual stance is evidenced almost from the moment of his entrance into the space of the narrative— when he throws wide the door separating his office from Dutchy's bar and orders Joe to take up the next mail run. Joe introduces Bonnie; and Jeff, promptly and self-consciously, confirms Joe's orders and assigns Les the all-night job of checking over some new equipment (Les: "When did you think that up?" Jeff: "Just now.") thus asserting an oppressive and disregardful sort of sexual prerogative. More important than what Jeff does, however, is his overbearing and insulting manner of doing it. He strides up to the table, without removing his wide-brimmed hat (itself an icon of power and oppressiveness: he's hatless at film's end); he takes Bonnie's cigarette from her hand, without asking, to light his own (she finally grabs his hand and takes it back); he positions himself "above" the still-seated Bonnie, putting his left leg up on what had been Joe's chair; and he responds to her assertion that she has "something to say" about Jeff's joining her for dinner with a demeaning question ("Chorus girl?") uttered around the cigarette which hangs insultingly from the corner

Cary Grant as Jeff Carter in Only Angels Have Wings.

of his mouth—all of which Hawks emphasizes by use of extreme close–ups which underline Jeff's sexual cynicism and the self-assertiveness of Bonnie's response.

To this point, to be certain, we are unaware of Jeff's sexual history—but Jeff's method of dealing with that history becomes clear when we compare Jeff's initial response to Bonnie with his response to the next woman boat-passenger he meets, whose arrival coincides with that of McPherson and his wife at the beginning of the film's second section. Jeff is all smiles and affection—even if he cannot remember names and places: was it Lola in Panama or Felicia in Puerto Rico? And the point is clear: Jeff is far more comfortable with women he can leave (or has left) behind. It is not that he doesn't like women—notice how quickly he sets his sights on Bonnie—but he likes women he is unlikely to get seriously involved with. Hence the appropriateness for Jeff of Baranca as a setting: he can always put a woman on the next boat out or can escape by taking up the next mail run.

It is arguable, moreover, that Jeff's fear of women is not a fear of women alone, or even of women per se; the issue, rather, has to do with mortality in general. That is, Jeff's fear of women can be read as a fear of the biological facts which women represent to men: aging, death, and reproduction. In fact, it is frequently the case in Hawks that his action-film protagonists are adolescents in some sense who strive mightily to avoid growing up—and the characters of *Only Angels Have Wings* are fairly typical in this respect. In some films this refusal to mature takes the form of a dedication to the past, often, as in *The Dawn Patrol* (1930) and *The Big Sky* (1952), a dedication to the memory of a dead brother. We see this in *Only Angels* in the grudge that Kid holds against McPherson: it was Kid's brother who went down with the plane after Bat bailed out. Another version of this dedication involves loyalty to a deceased father or father figure: it is the memory of his father's martyrdom at the hands of the landowners that drives Pancho Villa to banditry and revolution in *Viva Villa!* (1934) and it is out of loyalty to Johnny Diamond that the James Caan character in *El Dorado* (1967) seeks revenge. A third variant of this denial of time and mortality can be seen in films like *The Criminal Code* (1931) and *Scarface*, where it takes the form of implicitly incestuous sexual relations: thus the Walter Huston character in *Criminal Code* treats his daughter like a wife, as if her mother had not died or never existed; and Tony Camonte in *Scarface* expresses his implicit fear of adulthood by attempting to deny, if not to monopolize, the sexuality of his sister.

More commonly, however, the fear of maturity is expressed through the metaphor of male partnership or brotherhood. Such "male relationships" are not a priori negative. To the extent that they encourage mutual action and mutual concern they are positive in Hawks. But it is generally the case that the men use such relationships, like Jeff Carter in *Only Angels Have Wings*, as a retreat from the facts of temporality and sexuality. Thus in *The Crowd Roars* (released in 1932 and derived, like *Only Angels*, from an original Hawks story) the James Cagney character uses racing as an excuse to avoid marriage and to maintain his "hero" status in respect to his younger brother, Eddie (Eric Linden). Indeed, the film begins with Cagney's return home, as if he were seeking to recapture or reaffirm his boyhood courage by reasserting his "big brother" relationship with Eddie. But Eddie, whom Joe does not even recognize upon arrival, refuses to stay locked into the younger brother role for long. He insists upon growing up, both as a racer and as a husband to the Joan Blondell character. And hence Joe Greer's attempt to deny his own mortality and sexuality comes back eventually to haunt him. He would rather run his brother off the track than see him win—and Joe's madness results in the death of the Frank McHugh character, who serves in the film as an exemplary alternative to Cagney's denial of sexual and temporal reality: Spud is married and the father of a son. Joe Greer thus wants to deny temporal fact—even if that means "killing" fact by killing Spud. At the same time, however, Spud's death, and specifically the smoke and the stench from his doomed racing car, provides Joe with an unforgettable image of the temporality of human circumstances—and it is only by facing that reality, with the help of his fiancee (Ann Dvorak) and his brother, that he manages to overcome his fears of living, loving, and racing.

Like Joe Greer, then, Jeff Carter in *Only Angels Have Wings* evidences a certain fear of temporality, as expressed not only through his relationships with Bonnie and Judy but through his choice of place and profession and through his choice of comrades as well. Indeed, by playing "Papa" to men who are either his contemporaries or his elders Jeff effectively attempts to deny the facts and implications of paternity and sexuality by reversing their terms: the older you become the younger you get—it's the oldest flyer who is "The Kid."

In this respect it is interesting to consider the flying sequences in *Only Angels Have Wings* (the title itself raises the temporality issue) as they help us to reflect upon the relationship in the film between human fears and natural processes. The standard view of Hawks's adventure films tends to treat such action sequences in terms of the issue of professionalism—thus Joe Souther dies in the first flying scene because (as Jeff puts it to Dutchy) "he wasn't good enough." He didn't have the professional (and moral) know-how to "conquer" nature and that failure results from his attraction to Bonnie: Joe defies orders to circle the field because he fears Bonnie will be gone before he lands. And a similar professional failure is a contributing factor in the aborted and fatal mail-run undertaken by Bat and Kid: when they can't fly over the mountains Kid defies orders and tries to take the plane through the pass blind, only to run into a flock of condors—so once again nature (birds/woman) conquers mankind, or so this line of argument goes.

It is readily demonstrable, however, that this man versus nature opposition cannot account for what takes place. Rather, the two crashes represent less a failure to conquer nature so much as a failure to *trust* nature sufficiently, a failure which is clearly analogous to Jeff's inability to trust women. Joe does not believe the fog will clear in time for him to land and dine with Bonnie—so he tries to fly through it. But before Bonnie leaves the weather does clear, not completely, to be sure, but enough to allow Jeff to complete the mail run. Likewise, the second crash is attributable to failures of trust: Kid does not consider the possibility of waiting out the fog (in this he repeats Joe's mistake) and his eagerness reflects in part his distrust of and disgust for Bat. Thus it is thematically appropriate that Kid's moral rigidity in regards to McPherson should result in a broken neck: Kid was, quite literally, too inflexible for his own good. Furthermore, it's colliding with the condors that is the immediate cause of the crash; and it's significant that the condors represented no real threat to the flyers until after Jeff expresses his distrust of nature by accepting Tex's suggestion and ordering Bat to drop the nitro on them. Jeff thus loses a friend precisely *because* he distrusts the natural world—not the contrary.

It is all the more significant, therefore, that Bat McPherson should be the one to bring the crippled tri-motor back to the field—precisely because he has demonstrated a greater measure of trust and flexibility, both in respect to loving and flying. He is the only married flyer of the group, and he is the only flyer willing and able to take the tough jobs. He's the one who agrees to bring out the mine-owner's son, a task he accomplishes by trusting to physical law (gravity), both to decrease his air speed on landing (he comes in from *below* the edge of the plateau and drops down as soon as he clears it) and to gain speed and lift on takeoff (when he plunges off the cliff's edge and gains velocity enough to pull out of the dive). Of course, it is Bat who drops the nitro on the condors, and he suffers for it; but clearly he is less at fault in this regard than Jeff, who gives the order and suffers the greater loss in losing Kid.

We have already remarked upon the structural regularity of *Only Angels Have Wings*, on the fact that each of its three main sections shares a common outline of action, and we have seen how this regularity of structure serves in part to raise the issue of trust, both in matters of sex and flying. Thus Jeff's flying—and his operation of the flying service—can be seen as a denial of sexual vulnerability; but his flying, like Bat's, can also be seen to imply a positive capacity to accept vulnerability. Indeed, before Bat's arrival Jeff had taken on the really dangerous missions himself. The primary emotional question, then, for most of the characters in the film, involves the creation or continuation of trust, in the world and in each other—and the film's repetitive structure, while helping to pose the problem, also helps to promote its solution. More specifically, the film's structure of repeated incident allows characters (and ourselves as viewers) to see similar events from different physical and emotional perspectives, in a manner analogous to that in which Hawks's camera assumes a variety of perspectives in "describing" the initial entry of the tramp steamer into the port of Baranca.

The importance of perspective is emphasized repeatedly in the film, both in its dialogue and action and in the blocking and framing of sequences. We have already encountered the perspective issue relative to dialogue in the language-play of the film's opening sequence: our ability to understand the dialogue of the scene hinged upon our ability to read it in context. The same can be said for much of the film's dialogue, which serves repeatedly if implicitly to remind us that we need to see things in their totality. Thus Jeff's remark to Dutchy that Joe "wasn't good enough," for example, ought not to be read (though it often is) as a straightforward and unqualified statement of the film's theme. It is clear, rather, that Jeff says it specifically in the context of his own and Dutchy's grief, and when Dutchy quite properly wonders why Jeff sent Joe up (if he "wasn't good enough") Jeff drops the ability issue and replies: "What, ground that kid? Say, he'd sooner be where he is than quit." The ability issue is further qualified or undercut only a few moments later when Bonnie herself confronts Jeff over the matter of Joe's death: to her he replies that it was her fault, and Dutchy's, Jeff's own fault, the fog's fault, even the tree's fault—no mention is made of Joe's failure. The point to make here, however, is less that Joe failed than that Jeff does his agonized best to give both Dutchy and Bonnie the answer each needs, to see things from his or her point of view.

Far more explicit references to the perspective issue, both reflecting the contradictory qualities of Jeff Carter's personality, his intuitive human insight on the one hand and his distrust of women on the other, are evidenced in the advice that Jeff gives to Bonnie, soon after Joe's death in part one, and to Judy, after Bat flies the nitro run later in the film. In both cases Jeff quite correctly points to the fact that neither woman has taken full enough account of the male viewpoint. Thus Jeff responds to Bonnie's hysteria over the group's reaction to Joe's death by asking her to see it their way: "If you feel like bawling, how do you think we feel?" And he responds to Judy's drunken cynicism, the result of her inability to get Bat to reveal the reason for his ostracism from the other flyers, by urging her to see Bat's side of it. As Jeff puts it to her, if it is "so bad he can't tell you, how do you think he feels?" In both cases, however, Jeff is not content to state the general principle in terms such that it applies equally to everyone, himself included. On the contrary, in each instance it becomes an opportunity to justify his own detachment: thus he concludes his advice to Bonnie by ushering her out the bar-room door, and he tells Judy that her inability "to stick" has removed any doubts he might have had about bailing out of their earlier relationship. One measure of the progress of the film's narrative, then, is precisely the degree to which Jeff opens himself up to the vulnerability which he urges upon the women, on his ability, that is, to accept the validity of the woman's point of view, granting to her the same prerogative for risk taking which he naturally assumes for himself; and we can judge that progress on Jeff's part by reference to blocking and framing in the two crash-and-aftermath sequences.

The first such sequence, involving Joe Souther's death, is characterized by the gap, both spatial and metaphorical, between Jeff's point of view and Bonnie's. Once it is clear that Joe will be returning to the field Jeff and Kid leave the office and go to the radio box at the field's edge, where they occupy the foreground of the film frame. Bonnie, with Les and Dutchy, follows behind but stops short, taking a position in the background, screen left. The separateness of their positions will gain further emphasis through cutting, which tends to separate foreground and background; but the point to make is that Jeff has his back to Bonnie and is at some distance from her: she cannot see the emotion on Jeff's face while he tries to talk Joe down or after Joe crashes, cannot see the anguished expression as Kid lights and passes a cigarette to Jeff. And by the time Bonnie does get a good face-to-face look at Jeff, across the dinner table, after Jeff has talked to Dutchy in the office, Jeff has regained his iron-man composure—hence Bonnie's frustration.

The spatial coordinates in the second crash/aftermath sequence are quite different, particularly in respect to the relationship of Jeff and Bonnie. There is no sense that Jeff is hiding his emotions from her. She is part of the crew surrounding Jeff in his office while the doctor works on his shoulder. Likewise, Bonnie stands right beside (though slightly behind) Jeff as they gather around the dying Kid Dabb in the darkness of the repair shed. And Bonnie is right there when Jeff buys Bat a drink at Kid's behest. Furthermore, Jeff makes no real attempt, some few moments later, after Kid's effects are brought in and spread on the bar, to hide from Bonnie the agony he feels at Kid's death. The very fact that he walks out of the bar with Kid's effects in hand is in itself an explicit acknowledgment of his own vulnerability; and that he only goes as far as his office (rather than, say, to his room) amounts to an acknowledgment that he needs human contact, especially Bon-

Intimate space: Cary Grant and Jean Arthur as Jeff and Bonnie.

nie's. As Sparks puts it to her, when she wonders whether to go in and say goodbye (her boat is set to leave): "I think he'd want you to." And finally, when Bonnie enters the office Jeff makes no effort to hide or excuse his tears. Rather, he allows Bonnie to share his most intimate space, his office, the closeup frame, his grief itself—at which point the weather suddenly clears, as if in acknowledgment of Jeff's new-found ability to trust his feelings and to trust Bonnie. Indeed, it is precisely his ability to trust Bonnie which is celebrated when Jeff gives her Kid's two-headed coin: he knows she'll be able to see "both sides" and will understand the gift, in its context, as an invitation to stay.

To the extent that *Only Angels Have Wings* is typical of Hawks's adventure films—and critics are fairly unanimous in agreeing that the film draws "together the main thematic threads of Hawks's work"[5]—we are now in a position to critique certain elements of the generally accepted description of the Hawksian world view. It is clearly the case, for example, that Peter Wollen's analysis of character dynamics in the adventure films, regarding the relationships of characters to each other, to society, and to nature, is remarkably inaccurate and misleading when applied to *Only Angels*.

We have already considered the latter relationship, that of characters to nature in *Only Angels Have Wings*, and have seen the issue to be less a matter of man conquering nature than of overcoming his distrust of it. I will return to this point.

Furthermore, it is not true of *Only Angels Have Wings*, or most of the previous or subsequent adventure films, that the cast of characters is exclusively male in some positive sense, though males certainly have an edge in numbers. In fact, the exclusion of women as a thematic issue generally runs parallel to some other sort of interpersonal, usually male-typical brutality—and it's the men who undergo the real testing in Hawks, not the women. On the contrary, it is usually the case, as in *Only Angels*, that women are quite readily accepted into the group by everyone *except* the ostensible hero, and his refusal either to accept the woman or to acknowledge her sexual integrity reflects generally upon the hero's insufficiency, not hers—as can be seen in films as diverse as *Tiger Shark* (1932), *Come and Get It* (1936), *Rio Bravo* (1959), and *Hatari!* (1962), to name only a few.

It is also inaccurate to describe *Only Angels*, or the adventure films generally, as antisocial in the sense that characters in the films are to be seen as rejecting established society in some positive and unqualified manner. On the contrary, as in *Only Angels Have Wings*, the rejection of established society can often be read negatively, as an expression of egocentrism or immaturity. Thus in *Ceiling Zero* (1936), for example, it's the barnstorming egocentrism of the James Cagney character that is called into question—while Pat O'Brien does the best job he can of running his commercial aviation service safely without being disloyal to his professionally and sexually irresponsible friend.

In addition, it is also true that "professionals" in Hawks, though professionals for largely personal reasons, are generally involved in activities which have positive social consequences. The fishermen in *Tiger Shark*, for instance, are part of a large ethnic community and their fishing serves to nurture that community, both physically and socially. Both *Ceiling Zero* and *Only Angels* involve air-mail flying services: in each film the flyers serve a positive social function, a "communications" function. (This "communication" motif is picked up in certain comedies, *His Girl Friday* [1940] and *Ball of Fire* [1941], for example, where the central characters are journalists and scholars, respectively.) Even in *The Big Sky* (1952), where the basic movement of the film is clearly outward, away from society, the trading expedition has positive social consequences for breaking the monopolistic hold of the trading company represented by Streak. And the same can be said of all the "trilogy" Westerns, where the protagonists, whether lawmen (as in *Rio Bravo* and *El Dorado*) or ex–army officers (*Rio Lobo*), are also pitted against monopoly capitalists of one sort or another. Perhaps the best examples in Hawks of characters who work for the good or sake of society are the protagonists in his war films. In some instances they are at the front, at some physical remove from the society they are defending, as in *The Dawn Patrol* (1930) and *Air Force* (1943). But far more often that society is pictured in considerable detail, as in *Today We Live* (1933), *Viva Villa!*, *Sergeant York*, and *To Have and Have Not* (1944). The striking thing to note, however, is that in only one of the latter group of films is America the society being defended—and the society in that one, *Sergeant York,* is primitive and individualistic, very much like the societies in the Westerns.

Such descriptive errors, however, are in certain respects of secondary importance: one only needs to see enough films to recognize the inaccuracies. More crucial are the interpretive errors which result from and are encouraged by such factual distortions. And the chief interpretive error, especially in respect to the adventure films, is that which describes the world view of Howard Hawks as being essentially bitter and tragic.

Ultimately, this, too, is a perspective issue, having to do with the relationship in the films between thematic/visual background and dramatic foreground, between the circumstances of characters and the values their actions serve to celebrate. One way of characterizing that relationship is in terms of opposition. Thus for Peter Wollen the tension is one between death, which renders life in Hawks meaningless, and the action of the group; or, put another way, the tension is between the natural universe, as an implicit and hostile agent of death, and human beings, who assert an existential conquest of death and nature by means of their professionalism. The visual expression of this background conflict would then be, as Robin Wood in discussing *Only Angels Have Wings* describes it, "the single light that emphasises the darkness around"—at which point we could describe the whole film, as Wood describes the peanut vendor song sung by Bonnie and Jeff soon after Joe Souther's death, as being a "shout of defiance in the face of the darkness surrounding human life and the chaos of the universe" (21).

I find very little in *Only Angels Have Wings*—or in Hawks's adventure films generally—which would support this contention that the universe of Howard Hawks is in itself active and essentially hostile or chaotic or dark in any consistently negative sense. The best evidence anywhere in Hawks of a hostile cosmos is in *The Thing* (1951), for which he did not claim directorial credit and which I find very peripheral to my understanding of Hawks's career as a whole; but even here the extraterrestrial monster is less hostility personified than a catalyst for the conflict between the airmen and the scientists, as the sharks are catalysts of the personal conflicts in *Tiger Shark*, for example. It is not that there isn't considerable hostility or chaos or darkness in the world of Hawks's films, but that in nearly every case its negativity is largely attributable to or is reflective of human sources or agents. Thus both of the crashes in *Only Angels Have Wings*, for example, are attributable not to nature but to human beings who are too caught up in their own plans to trust nature sufficiently enough. Indeed, the greatest threat to the flyers in *Only Angels Have Wings* is the contract deadline which forces Jeff to push his men and planes to their limits: again, hostility has its origins in human plans. It is only if one considers death a priori an expression of universal hostility that it is possible to maintain the view that men and nature are opposed to one another in *Only Angels Have Wings*. In this respect, indeed, we can appeal to iconography to support the claim that life and death in the world of *Only Angels*, and in the world of Hawks's films generally, are to be seen as complements rather than opposites, points on the same continuum of experience rather than opposed terms which cancel each other out.

The iconographic systems in *Only Angels Have Wings* bearing most directly on the issue of the relationship between man and nature are those involving light and water. And clearly both sorts of imagery are associated in the film with death. Joe Souther cannot land because the fog is so thick that searchlights cannot cut through it—and this light/dark opposition is reinforced by the image of the circular tin lamp hanging over the field-side radio box, casting a diffuse cone of light around Jeff and Kid as they try to communicate with Joe. Likewise, Kid Dabb's death scene is played by the light from a single kerosene lantern while rain washes down a window in the background.

But it is equally true that water and light in *Only Angels Have Wings* are associated with positive sexuality as well. Indeed, the whole opening section of the film employs a visual rhetoric of

Sternbergian sexual romanticism, which associates mist and light very clearly with sexual adventure, and this association is quite explicitly reinforced through the course of the film. Thus the earliest example of the circle of light surrounded by darkness (excluding the lighted portholes of the steamer) is seen in the native cafe, where it is associated with sexuality and community. And the low-hanging conical lamps are fixtures throughout the film, especially in Dutchy's bar (which is frequently full of men *and* women) and in Jeff's bedroom. Indeed, Hawks turns those lamps into icons of continuity by cutting "around" them, so that they serve to anchor our sense of space by their placement in the frame.

Water, likewise, serves a similarly positive function in *Only Angels Have Wings*. Thus Jeff uses ice water to clear his head before taking up the mail in part one and to clear Judy's head later on when he advises her to see Bat's side of things. And the key scene between Jeff and Bonnie in his bedroom begins with Jeff's coming out of the rain to find Bonnie in the bath: water for both is thus associated with a cleansing sort of emotional honesty, and this association is reinforced when a rain-soaked Judy comes through the door a few minutes later to thank Jeff for his advice. It's as if rain has the effect in the film of bringing characters to their physical and sexual senses—hence the appropriateness of the final few frames wherein Les and Jeff take up the last mail run while Bonnie watches from the office porch: rain washes the image throughout the sequence, binding the characters together in a continuous emotional and temporal space despite the back-and-forth rhythm of the cutting.

Indeed, in this focus on the continuity of sexual and professional action, the world view of *Only Angels Have Wings*, and of Hawks's films generally, is far better described as comic than tragic, and this is true in two respects. To begin with, as Robin Wood and John Belton both point out, there is the "innate flexibility and durability of [Hawks's] characters."[6] It is almost always the Hawks case, and particularly in his post-1930s films, that his characters manage to survive both their circumstances and their own mistakes. Thus, as Robin Wood remarks, "by the end of *Only Angels Have Wings* almost every character has undergone a process of improvement" (21). Both Bonnie and Jeff have gained a new ability to take risks, Bonnie in loving Jeff, Jeff in loving Bonnie. And the same can be said for Bat and Judy: both redeem themselves through selfless action. Dutchy, furthermore, is rescued (or soon will be) from financial ruin—so that the flying service will continue operating. Even Kid Dabb, it is implied, dies a better man. He is purged of his bitterness toward McPherson; and he dies, like Joe Souther, as a pilot ("He'd sooner be where he is than quit"). More significantly, *Only Angels* is also comic in another sense—in the sense that it takes place, like most of Hawks's films, in what must be described, on balance, as a positively benevolent universe. Even where human action results in tragic consequences—in *Wings* the deaths of Joe and Kid—the Hawksian cosmos is generally characterized by benevolent coincidences which repeatedly and consistently give people the second chances they need to work through their past mistakes. In the professional world of *Only Angels Have Wings*, for example, it is probably no great coincidence that Bat McPherson should show up at Baranca, where Kid Dabb works for Dutchy and Jeff. But that he shows up married to Jeff's ex–girl friend, and at precisely the time when Bonnie arrives, is a benevolent coincidence of the first order: every one of these characters is necessary to work through the film's emotional issues. And they are there when they are needed—as they are repeatedly in Hawks. Of course, it is exactly that sort of coincidence that Hawks's critics often pass off as melodramatic convention—hence, for example, the dissatisfaction with the ending of *Red River* (1948) or with almost all of *Red Line 7000* (1965), wherein the matter of luck is a central thematic concern—but the Hawksian universe on the whole is a universe of second chances and comic good fortune. Only in films like *The Dawn Patrol* and *Scarface* where human beings take fortune too much into their own hands, whether willingly or not, do things work differently, and even in those films characters often receive unexpected opportunities to redeem themselves (as Courtney does in *The Dawn Patrol* when the order comes down to undertake the solo bombing run). On balance, however, the world view of the adventure films is benevolently comic—and *Only Angels Have Wings* is no exception to the rule.

Hawksian Comedy: *I Was a Male War Bride* (1949)

To suggest, however tentatively, that the world view of *Only Angels Have Wings*, and of Hawks's adventure films generally, is positive or comic is only to disagree in part with the standard view of Hawks: even Sarris has suggested that the adventure films represent the more positive aspect of the Hawksian vision. Thus it is in the comedies, as Sarris and Wollen and others would have it, that the bitterness of the Hawksian world view is more clearly expressed.

Indeed, chaos in the comedies is very directly personified in the figure of the madcap Hawksian female—who comes to represent a double threat to the often fragile or unsure masculinity of the comic Hawksian hero: on the one hand she is natural sexuality in its most demanding and debilitating form, leaving the hero no choice but ego-threatening submission; and on the other she represents the stultifying demands of society and domesticity, asserting "the power of the monogamous-minded woman over the sexually independent male" (Murphy, 280).

It must be said in advance that this general view of Hawks's comedies is problematic, if only because the comedies lend themselves far less readily to this sort of broad generalization than do the adventure films. To begin with, the comedies, while numerous, are spotted throughout the canon and are often more fruitfully read in the context provided by the adventure films of the same period than in the context of the comedies taken a-chronologically as a group. In addition, to describe the plot action of the comedies as the domination of woman over man ignores the quite obvious fact that in two of the comedies, *Twentieth Century* (1934) and *His Girl Friday,* it's somewhat the other way around (Oscar Jaffe and Walter Burns being the prime aggressors in their films)—or the fact that in certain (if not most) of the comedies the dynamics of male/female interaction are far more evenly balanced than the standard view implies: thus in *Ball of Fire,* for example, it's the Barbara Stanwyck character who undergoes the greatest change, while in *Monkey Business* (1952) the reversion to childhood is mutually experienced and mutually beneficial. Furthermore, it must also be noted that the comedies exhibit a striking diversity in matters of pacing and characterization, ranging from the madcap characters and momentum of *Twentieth Century* and *Bringing Up Baby* to the far more relaxed and reflective pacing and characterizations of films like *Fig Leaves* (1926), *Ball of Fire,* and *Man's Favorite Sport?* (1964). The whole picture can be even more complicated if one chooses to include among the comedies certain of the adventure films. *Hatari!,* for example, is frequently discussed in this context, and I would go so far as to include films like *The Crowd Roars, Only Angels Have Wings,* and *The Big Sleep* (1946) in the category. One must therefore be all the more careful and cautious in discussing the comedies, as opposed to the adventure films, so as to avoid overgeneralizing to the point of falsehood.

All of which said, I am perfectly willing to agree with the general contention that *I Was a Male War Bride* is the "darkest" of Hawks's comedies, "one of his bleakest, blackest, and most serious works."[7] If nothing else, *War Bride* is bleak to the extent that it corresponds more thoroughly than any other Hawks comedy to the standard model, of female dominance and male humiliation, proposed by Peter Wollen—to which we will return. But this general quality of "bleakness" is evident, as both Robin Wood and John Belton have described the film, at several other levels of the text, especially in its backgrounds, its mise-en-scène, and its dialogue.

According to Wood, "an oppressive dinginess hangs over the whole film"—and is a function both of setting ("military offices, bare corridors, dark inn-room") and of lighting (much of the film taking place in darkness or at night).[8] The first of these associations, equating drabness or lifelessness with the visual and thematic background provided by military bureaus and bureaucracies, is clearly central to our understanding of the film. The credit sequence, which features traveling footage of Free-French Captain Henri Rochard (Cary Grant) being driven through the streets of an unidentified German city, is photographed against a background of bombed-out buildings and rubble—and when he arrives at Heidelberg it is in part to enter into a mazelike series of ill-lit hallways which force him to rely upon a woman, WAC Lieutenant Catherine Gates (Ann Sheridan), for directions. And one can chart the general movement of the film, particularly after Gates and Rochard are married, by reference to place or setting: for Henri especially marriage begins as an exasperating journey from one military billet to the next—and repeatedly the Catherine-less Henri is told "you can't sleep here."

The progress of the main characters through the narrative can be read, therefore, as a series of progressively more problematic confinements at the hands of the military establishment. Against his will and hers (or so it seems), Henri is assigned Catherine as his interpreter. Against his will Henri is forced to ride in the sidecar while Gates pilots the cycle (Henri is not "checked out" to drive cycles himself). Henri is accidentally locked in Catherine's room at the inn in Baden-Auheim, and spends the night (or most of it) trying to sleep in an upright wooden chair. In the morning Henri goes "undercover" by changing clothes with the much smaller innkeeper, in order to contact a black-market lens-grinder (his ostensible mission); and he is arrested and jailed when Catherine, obeying his express and unqualified order to deny knowledge of him or his mission, refuses to identify Henri to the German police. And once they are married Henri and Catherine suffer confinement of an even greater magnitude, the confinement of the impulse toward marital affection, a confinement brought about by physical separation. Thus their wedding night is interrupted when Catherine receives orders shipping her back to Heidelberg from Paris. They are then refused lodgings at Henri's Bachelor Officer's Quarters and at six different hotels (as they tell the tale to Kitty). At Kitty's they sleep apart, Catherine with Kitty, Henri in the bathtub. And once they arrive in Bremerhaven, their point of embarkation for the states, Henri spends the night trying to find a place to sleep, to no avail.

This sense of physical and emotional confinement is further reinforced in the film's mise-en-scène and, more ominously, in its dialogue. As John Belton points out, the progress of the film's narrative is punctuated at crucial moments by three shots—which suggest "Rochard's entrapment and powerlessness by framing him . . . between two other characters," usually Catherine standing to one side, and some representative of the army or the American bureaucracy on the other (27). The emblematic significance of such shots is fairly clear: Henri is caught between the desire for (or fear of) sexuality on the one hand and military or bureaucratic regulations on the other. And the possible consequence of this sort of physical and visual entrapment is alluded to in the film's dialogue, where the matters of sexual identity and physical mutilation are repeatedly brought up.

The identity issue, of course, is explicit in the film's title: *I Was a Male War Bride*. And most of the sexual wordplay arises from the conflict between the bureaucratic expectation that war brides will be female and the indisputable truth of Henri Rochard's maleness— despite the fact that "public law 271 of the Congress" makes no sexual distinctions. Thus Henri is repeatedly called upon to explain his status to various military paper shufflers: "According to the War Department I *am* my wife." And hence as well Henri's gratitude when his maleness is finally acknowledged by one of his fellow war brides, who willingly admits that the screaming bundle in her arms "is a baby" while Henri "is a man." All of which carries ominous implications when seen in the context of the mutilation imagery which is replete in the film's dialogue. Henri at one point, for example, had threatened to tear Catherine's head off and make her eat it; she subsequently warns him that she'll carry a trench knife on their mission to ward off his advances ("If you so much as lay a finger on me this trip you're going back to France minus a lot of parts you probably value"); and she also refers to Henri as Jack the Ripper. The correlation in the dialogue of mutilation with the loss of sexual identity is thus quite explicit—so much so that Henri is understandably leery when the American consul, speaking in reference to the immigration forms, talks of "making the proper adjustments."

One can readily see how certain aspects of *I Was a Male War Bride* lend themselves to a Wollenesque reading of the film as expressing a bitter view of human life and sexuality. If the basic impulse of the Hawksian female is to humiliate and de-sex her man in the service of social decorum then it is possible to read the progress of the *War Bride* narrative as an implicit process of sexual mutilation which culminates when Catherine dresses Henri up as a WAC lieutenant in order to smuggle him aboard the homebound troop ship. Indeed, early in the film it is Catherine who wears the pants (when she pilots the cycle), and certain critics, especially Robin Wood and Kathleen Murphy, are convinced that she never relinquishes the implicit desire to "reduce [Henri] to impotence" (Murphy, 280). As Wood puts it: "Lieutenant Gates is Hawks's extremest and most explicit portrait of the modern American female, aggressive and domineering, determinedly subjugating the male" and "gloating over her husband's discomfitures" (85, 87).

The logic necessary to support this general view of the film and its significance, however, is extremely shaky and is only partially supported by the evidence of the film.

To begin with, it is a gross oversimplification to suggest that the sexual dynamics of *I Was a Male War Bride* are completely one dimensional: the female conquers and the male submits. If there is any place in the film where one character consciously and maliciously sets out to sexually humiliate the other it is Henri who does the humiliating—and yet even that act, his waltzing into Gates's office and ceremoniously delivering her underwear to her one garment at a time, naming each piece of clothing aloud and in turn, cannot be read as an act of simple-minded callousness. If anything, despite the obvious pleasure he gets out of making Catherine look foolish, he also clearly enjoys her reaction and her presence—witness the knowing smile which crosses his face when they get out into the hallway and she calls him a "stinker." Put another way, if he were serious about having nothing more to do with Gates, he would not go so far out of his way to throw down the sexual gauntlet (the same can be said, parenthetically, of Hildy Johnson in *His Girl Friday*: her telling Walter she's getting married is an implicit challenge for him to reassert himself as her husband).

By contrast, the only time in *I Was a Male War Bride* when Gates even half tries to make Henri look foolish is when Rochard is arrested and she refuses to identify him. But his "humiliation" in this case is far

Sexual gamesmanship: Cary Grant delivers Ann Sheridan's underwear in I Was a
Male War Bride.

more his doing than hers. She had nothing to do with his foolish
costume, and in refusing to identify him she follows his quite empha-
tic and unqualified orders. In this case it's Henri who acts the military
bureaucrat and he gets an appropriate comeuppance in return. To be
sure, Catherine does take over the mission. With the help of two male
officers (it is not an exclusively "female" plot) she finds the lens-
grinder Henri had been looking for. But her motive for doing so,
clearly, is concern for Henri, not a desire to emasculate him. She
knew it was his last mission and does her best to be helpful. Indeed, as
soon as she realizes that she's offended him she apologizes.

    That one incident aside, however, and there is not a single moment
in the film where Catherine tries to make Henri look foolish. To be
sure, Henri looks foolish quite often. And Catherine's response is
always healthy, generous, unmalicious laughter and smiles. But Henri's foolishness is usually a function of his refusal to pay attention to the
world around him, a failure clearly related to his refusal to acknowledge his feelings toward Catherine or hers toward him. The best
example of this involves the moment when Henri almost rows their

boat over a dam because he refuses to heed Catherine's warning. But the same can be said of the incidents with the railway gate, the newly painted sign pole, and even of the incident in Catherine's room at the inn with the chair that he tries to sleep on—it never occurs to Henri that he might simply stretch out on the floor. Indeed, his gymnastic attempt to sleep in the upright chair is evidence not only of a hopeful physical resiliency but of his inflexible attitude toward Catherine as well. The only instance in the film where one of Henri's serious pratfalls is *not* primarily his own fault is when the innkeeper's wife shoves him off the awning outside Catherine's window. Yet even here it is not a matter of Catherine seeking to humiliate him. Rather, she fears her own humiliation and Henri's response once again evidences an implicit concern for her feelings. If he didn't at some level care for her he'd simply stay put and let Catherine suffer the embarrassment of being discovered with a man in her room.

It is far more accurate to describe the stormy relationship of Henri Rochard and Catherine Gates as a classic example of positive Hawksian "sex antagonism," as Catherine herself puts it to Henri. Their relationship is a long standing one, with a history of missions accomplished and sexual faux pas, and the key issues between them are extremely *personal* ones, his temperament and philandering, her sexual reticence in the face of his wine-induced ardor. But the fact of their genuine attraction for one another is evidenced very early on. Thus Henri goes out of his way to see Catherine again, despite his understanding that he will be assigned another, more sexually forward ("stacked" is his term) WAC interpreter for his next mission. Likewise, Catherine goes out of her way to tell her well-endowed WAC colleague that Henri uses maps instead of etchings to lure female victims into his Jack-the-Ripper clutches; and by so doing she both gets back at Henri for the underwear gag (both gags involve exaggerations of sexual fact) and she also—quite literally, in visual terms—"comes between" Henri and Lt. Billings, as if she were trying to frighten off a rival.

The key observation to make in respect to the relationship between Henri and Catherine is the obvious fact that Rochard and Gates (and Cary Grant and Ann Sheridan) clearly enjoy "playing off" each other. As with most Hawks couples, their courtship is as much intellectual—as expressed through their marvelously self-conscious and responsive wordplay and gesture-play—as it is purely erotic or physical (not that it isn't erotic and physical as well). Examples abound. Consider the moment when Henri and Catherine part com-

pany for the moment in the hallway of the Heidelberg headquarters.
They have just been discussing Henri's sexual proclivities and Henri's
parting comment is a question: "Why did you say I chase after
'everything in skirts'?" Catherine replies "I didn't" and begins to
move away; "I said 'anything.'" Rochard then deadpans "that's
different"—and then they both pause in mid-movement, Catherine
to look back over her shoulder, Henri to do a classic Cary Grant
double take as he looks over his shoulder at her. The whole routine
comes off as a beautifully timed and coordinated comic ballet between intellectual equals. Or, to take but one more example among
many, consider the scene in the chaplain's office where Henri and
Catherine are told that they will need to undergo three different
wedding ceremonies. Henri points out that in China "the bride and
groom just drink tea out of the same bowl"—at which point Catherine
takes her cue and together they launch into a delightful "who's on
first" routine which culminates in self-aware smiles and laughter.

It is remarkably inaccurate, then, to describe the Henri/Catherine
relationship as one sided or maliciously antagonistic. Rather, it is a
relationship based on mutual attraction and respect, by means of
which Hawks celebrates the integrity of mutually aware and mutually concerned sexual action. Indeed, it is only for the sake of further-
ing that action that Catherine is finally forced to dress Henri in WAC
drag—in order to get him aboard ship where they can finally consummate their marriage. And the gambit itself celebrates the ability
to respond to situations and to play with conventions. It is not being a
WAC alone that gets Henri aboard ship but the fact that Catherine
knows how to play on navy pride to usher Henri past the gangplank
sentries.

It is equally inaccurate to describe the social world of the film as
serving to express an unremittingly bleak view of experience—
though most of the bleakness in the film is attributable to overly-rigid
human attitudes and inflexible social conventions. I have already
outlined the case *against* society. By and large it is military bureaucracy in *I Was a Male War Bride* that keeps Henri and Catherine
apart after their wedding. And the logical outcome, should such
barriers to human sexuality be endlessly and mindlessly perpetuated,
would indeed be impotence—both personal and social. Hence the
many references to mutilation and castration. As Henri puts it to
Catherine, while they await approval of their marriage application,
"The American Army had better be careful or they're not going to
have any American children pretty soon." Such references to sterility

are not the whole film, however, and they serve primarily to make us aware of the value to be assigned to fruitful human relationships, of the sort eventually embodied by Henri and Catherine.

The real issue in the film is not even bureaucracy per se. Public law 271 of the Congress does in fact exist, quite specifically to promote the sexuality and fertility of American military personnel. The problem is that the military establishment misreads the law on the assumption that members of the military services are exclusively male and therefore that "spouses" of military personnel will be exclusively female. The effect, however inadvertent, is to deny the sexuality (if not the existence) of women like Catherine Gates. The social scheme of things is such that the sexual integrity of female military personnel is not even considered or taken account of. And it is in light of this disregard for female sexuality that we can understand the positive significance of Henri Rochard's sexual "transformation."

Through the first half of the film Henri's response to Catherine vacillates between explicit hostility and implicit affection, the affection expressed largely through physical gesture or action (rubbing her sore back or her cramped leg), the hostility expressed largely through dialogue. Specifically, Henri repeatedly tries to assert a dehumanizing linguistic and military prerogative. Thus when Catherine asks what she is supposed to do on their mission Henri replies: "To keep your mouth shut and do as I tell you." And once in Baden-Auheim he orders her not to speak to him, to pretend to complete ignorance of his person or mission, ostensibly in order to maintain his undercover persona, but his tone of voice in giving the order is very personal and sarcastic—and Henri's dehumanizing sarcasm is repaid in kind when Henri lands in jail.

It is therefore inaccurate to conclude that Henri's discomfiture in the second half of the film is unearned or unjust and is to be read as symptomatic of social or sexual hostility. Rather, it is the case that society in *I Was a Male War Bride* endeavors, however imperfectly, to encourage human sexuality; complications arise only when sexual integrity is denied. Thus in the first half of the film it is Henri who is the chief culprit, for insisting (however halfheartedly) that Catherine play the traditional female role, sexually available but professionally subservient; and in the film's second half Henri suffers appropriately in his turn, finding out at first hand what it means to be "a soldier's wife." And Henri is clearly a better man for the experience.

Finally, it is also inaccurate to assert that the "universe" of the film is ultimately bleak, tragic, or hostile. Those who argue the contention usually base their claim on twin assumptions: (1) that Catherine is a classic Hawksian madcap bent on reducing her man to impotence, and (2) that Catherine is representative of an equally hostile social bureaucracy. Neither assumption, as we have seen, is warranted and both fail to account for the degree to which Henri is responsible for his own dilemma.

Furthermore, one can argue in positive terms that the universe of *I Was a Male War Bride* is genuinely benevolent and comic. To begin with, the film invokes at certain key moments a Capraesque pastoral iconography reminiscent specifically of *It Happened One Night* (1934). Again we see rivers and haystacks; again we see sexual longing associated with wayside lodgings and rain washed windows. Indeed, the window shutters at the Baden-Auheim inn where Henri and Catherine seek shelter are decorated with valentine hearts. Thus the visual world of the film cannot be read exclusively, as it often is, in film-noir terms.

Comic benevolence finds its strongest expression, however, in an extravagant series of comic coincidences which enable Catherine and Henri to come to their emotional senses despite their mutual defensiveness. Thus Catherine is assigned to be Henri's interpreter despite his expectation to the contrary. Thus Catherine and Henri are on the verge of rowing over the falls when someone materializes on the bridge above and throws a rope to their boat so that together they can pull themselves to safety. Thus the handle of the door to Catherine's room comes off in Henri's hand, locking Henri in her room overnight and providing him opportunity to demonstrate respect for her sexual integrity. Thus while Catherine leaves the cycle to check directions children gather around Henri (now snoozing in the sidecar) and put the still running bike in gear—sending the driverless cycle down the road, across a field, and into a benevolently present haystack; and the incident is crucial for providing both Henri and Catherine an opportunity to see how much each matters to the other. Thus Catherine chases frantically after Henri and finds him frantically combing the haystack in search of his lost "darling"—he hadn't known she wasn't on the bike. One can even see the cross-dressing routine as evidence of a benevolent providence. No sooner is Henri thrown off the troopship than suddenly a statuesque WAC lieutenant appears and asks Catherine to hold her suitcase, thereby providing both the inspiration and the props for Henri's masquerade, a masquerade the end result of which is that Henri and Catherine are finally enabled to consummate their marriage.

All of which allows us to account for the fact that *I Was a Male War Bride* is an especially *delightful* film, far more so than its reputation as a "black comedy" would seem to indicate. Relationships in the film—of characters to each other, to society, and to nature—are alive and vital and fruitful. There is tension over the issue of trust, to be certain, a tension very much akin to that in *Only Angels Have Wings*: in both cases the sexual triviality of the Cary Grant character is called into question, both by his own deeper feelings and by the example of a sexually committed (though hardly emasculating) female. Taking human relationships seriously and responsibly is thus a risky business in Hawks, both in the adventure films and the comedies; but it is also exhilarating and rewarding. Indeed, it is exactly that sense of liberation and exhilaration which is captured in the film's sexually loaded closing image, the Statue of Liberty seen through the porthole of the cabin where Henri and Catherine have spent their honeymoon voyage making love. The shot resonates to a variety of connotations, chief among them the contrast with the Baden-Auheim bedroom scene (here they lock *themselves* in, thus taking responsibility for their

Liberty and sexuality: the final shot of I Was a Male War Bride.

relationship), but the dominant resonance is that of openly expressed
sexuality, on the part of the characters and on the part of the film
itself. And it is that sort of openness to experience which Hawks
celebrated throughout his career.

Conclusion

I have permitted myself to discuss *Only Angels Have Wings* and *I
Was a Male War Bride* at some length for two reasons: (1) because they
are two of Hawks's finest films, all of which reward and deserve this
sort of extended close analysis; and (2) because I wanted to demonstrate the degree to which the standard view of Hawks fails to account
in any thoroughgoing manner for the data of the films. Wollen's view
of Hawks attends only to the bare outlines of a select few Hawks films.
As soon as one attends closely to the whole complex of elements
which make up specific films the "Hawks-as-tragedian" view falls
apart. It is far more accurate, indeed, to describe the Hawksian world
view as comic; and the goal of this chapter has been to demonstrate
the plausibility of such a description even when it is applied to films
which are generally accounted among Hawks's "darkest" works. In
subsequent chapters I will continue to consider the validity of this
general approach to Hawks. But space limitations will require far
greater selectivity of example, in respect both to individual films and
to data from those films. It should remain clear, however, that the
ability to enrich our understanding of and response to specific films is
the ultimate measure of any critical act. The trouble with the standard
view of Hawks is that it forces us to ignore so much while seeing so
little.

3

Theme and Motif:
Hawks before Sound

AS MOLLY HASKELL POINTS OUT, only *A Girl in Every Port* (1928), among the films Hawks directed before the coming of sound, "has sustained more than marginal interest."[1] Partly this is the result of the lamentable fact that most of Hawks's presound films were long thought to be lost. Fortunately, however, many of them are now known to have survived. Another reason for this neglect, however, derives from the conviction, even on the part of scholars who apparently have seen the films, that, as Haskell goes on, "they have none of the qualities we associate with the later Hawks." As Jeffrey Richards also puts it, the surviving films are "wholly atypical of the mature Hawks," and they represent, in effect, "a period of apprenticeship and experimentation."[2]

It can hardly be said, it seems to me, that Hawks was an apprentice at the time he made his silent features—whether or not we take those films to be of a piece with his later work. Hawks directed his first film in 1925, the apparently lost *Road to Glory,* but he had been seriously and continuously involved with writing and producing films as early as 1922. It is unlikely, then, given the fact that production duties were far less rigidly defined during the early 1920s than they would be later, that Hawks was a total neophyte when he finally got the chance to direct his own scripts. Furthermore, the judgment that his early films are atypical (and therefore uninteresting) is founded, quite explicitly, on what I have termed the "standard" view of Hawks, derived from Bogdanovich, Wollen, et al. Indeed, Richards prefaces his entire *Focus on Film* discussion of "The Silent Films of Howard Hawks" with a capsule summary drawn quite directly from Wollen and Sarris.

My own view of the silent films is quite opposite. Even within the terms of the standard model these films can be seen to exhibit many of the themes and motifs which typify the later films. In this respect Hawks's tendency in interviews to disown or discount several of these films as having "no relation to [his] work" must be attributed either to poor memory or impatience.[3] This is especially true in the case of *Paid to Love* (1927), which Hawks described to Bogdanovich as a failed experiment in expressionistic camera work after Murnau. The Murnauesque moments in the film are few and far between, however; and in any case it can readily be argued that Hawks never let go of the expressionist heritage altogether. Certainly films like *Only Angels Have Wings* and *To Have and Have Not* continue to recall to mind the visual style of Murnau and of Von Sternberg; and even Hawks's later experiments with color, especially in *Man's Favorite Sport?* and *Red Line 7000,* can be seen to represent a logical extension of the expressionist premise. Thus there is nothing atypical about the fact that the silent films—like most Hawks films—evidence a strong sense of cinematic tradition while simultaneously expressing a world view which is consistently Hawksian. Indeed, the silent films are so typical that a discussion of several of them can serve as a general introduction to certain characteristic thematic and stylistic features of the Hawksian cinema.

Roles and Reversals

It is frequently observed that Hawks's plots, especially in the comedies, are characterized by various forms of "role reversal"—of male and female, of adult and child, of civilized and savage, etc. But the observation as typically expressed tends to limit the range of significance which can be attributed to such reversals. Thus the reversal is generally seen in negative terms, as a form of regression or humiliation, and accordingly characters are seen as victims of roles which are imposed upon them. It is exactly this view of the role reversal theme which dominates discussion of *I Was a Male War Bride,* for example. I believe it is demonstrable, however, that the ability of Hawksian characters to play roles, to reverse normal behavioral and social expectations, generally carries very positive connotations in the films, and is often a matter of conscious choice rather than external pressures. This is certainly true of several of the films Hawks wrote and/or produced before 1925. At least as described in the AFI catalog, for example, *Quicksands* (1923) and *Tiger Love* (1924) both key upon characters who consciously play roles for positive social ends.[4] Thus *Quicksands* involves a female undercover agent's attempt to break up a dope smuggling ring, while *Tiger Love* involves a Spanish Robin Hood who turns out to be an aristocrat. Indeed, it is generally true, as Jean Gili points out, that reversals in both the adventure films and the comedies result more in the restoration than the destruction of a healthy and self-aware equilibrium in personal and social relations.[5] Examination of some Hawks silents can illustrate the point.

The Cradle Snatchers (1927)

The Cradle Snatchers, though incompletely preserved, can nevertheless be read as a paradigm instance of role reversals and role playing in Hawks. Like many Hawks movies the film is structured in almost musical terms, as a sequence of themes and variations. That is, the film involves contrasting sets of characters—three young college boys and three older, upper-class couples—and contrasting sequences as well. Thus the film's first "movement" contrasts the sexual behavior of the three young men to that of the three husbands; the second movement, missing from the preserved print, apparently contrasts "real" sexuality with its "theatrical" counterpart (in that the three boys, at the urging of one's fiancée, attend a theater performance of a sexual melodrama); and the film's third movement involves the contrast between various forms of "cradle snatching": the wives "play around" with the college boys in order to cure the philandering of their flapper-fond husbands.

The "role reversals" involved are thus of two sorts: sexual/social and theatrical. And the interplay of the two is specified in the film's opening sequences—at the fraternity house, where the three college men are roommates, and at various mansions or townhouses, where the husbands prepare to step out on their wives. The problem in both sets of circumstances has to do with sex and/or money. One of the college boys, Oscar, is deathly afraid of women—he even hops hysterically onto a chair when a "woman" enters the room (anticipating Cary Grant in *Bringing Up Baby*, who hops onto a footstool when Baby enters the room). The other two college men are sexually active but financially strapped: Joe Valley ("a graduate sheik") asks Oscar for a loan to finance his amorous activities and Henry Winton is too broke to pay for the theater tickets he had promised his fiancée. The three husbands, on the other hand, are all well heeled—though here, too, money is related to some form of sexual dysfunction. That is, money enables all three men to deny the sexuality of their wives: they use

business as an excuse for going out alone and spending money on
their unappreciative flapper girl friends.

Such, then, is the situation at the film's beginning; and reversals of
a positive sort are subsequently brought about by the conscious
manipulation of theatricality. Thus Joe Valley, for example, sets about
to remedy his financial situation by enlisting the aid of Sam Ginsberg,
a member of the college drama club who excels in female impersonation. Sam goes into Oscar's room and faints into Oscar's arms—at
which point Joe enters and, amidst a flood of melodramatic gestures,
accuses Oscar of being "a fiend incarnate" for "despoiling" his
sweetheart, implying in the process that ten dollars would assuage his
agony. To be sure, Joe's ruse is not completely honest or to be
approved of, and Joe gets his comeuppance when Henry enters and
declares Sam to be his "sister." But the ingenuity of the gag is
undeniable and it serves Oscar right for being so vehemently afraid of
women.

More central to the film is the plot hatched by Ann Hall to stop the
"monkey business" of her philandering uncle and his philandering
cohorts. That the husbands deserve to be deceived as proposed by
Ann is established largely through the character of Ann's aunt, Kitty
Ladd—who continues to love her husband and is genuinely hurt by
his actions. Indeed, as a group the husbands are portrayed as being
childishly disregardful of the sexual needs of their wives. Accordingly, the deception itself functions to demonstrate, however comi-
cally, the legitimacy of those needs, to the wives themselves, to their
husbands, and to the college boys as well, especially Oscar. Thus the
final movement of the film finds Oscar, Joe, and Henry (Ann's fiancé)
arriving at the Ladd mansion to go through a dress rehearsal with the
wives of the masquerade intended to bring the husbands to their
sexual senses. And the theatrical context—which Hawks emphasizes
in his mise-en-scène by repeatedly framing characters against cur-
tains or doorways—allows various characters to experiment, to try
out various "styles" of sexuality. Thus Oscar and Ethel Drake both
undergo sexual initiations (Ethel: "I am just full of the joy of living");
while Joe and Susan Martin play the part of Latin lovers, Joe quite
consciously reenacting the first act of the play he had seen in the film's
second movement ("Husbands? What care Don Jose for husbands?").
At film's end, indeed, after the husbands come home unexpectedly to
find their wives dancing and carrying on, they, too, are told to get into
the act. As Susan Martin puts it to the husbands, as the wives and
college boys depart for a night on the town: "You thought we were

back numbers. We'll show you tonight that we're not. And while we're gone, for the love of Mike, learn some Spanish."

In *Cradle Snatchers*, then, we see several sorts of role reversal typical of later Hawks films: the reversal of age and youth (Oscar needs to act older, Ethel needs to act younger, the husbands need to act their age), the reversal of male and female (Sam plays the female role, the wives play at being cradle snatchers). But the pattern of those reversals is largely positive. If anything, it is the initial situation which is out of balance, in that characters (Oscar, the husbands) play roles either unconsciously or with too little regard for the feelings of others, and the subsequent reversals restore the balance by bringing characters to a more conscious awareness of their roles and responsibilities. Indeed, like many Hawks comedies (*Twentieth Century, Bringing Up Baby, Monkey Business, Man's Favorite Sport?*), *Cradle Snatchers* invokes an implicit analogy between the theatrical self-consciousness of the characters and the cinematic self-consciousness of the director. Thus no sooner does Susan Martin tell the husbands to learn some Spanish than Hawks uses a jump cut to transport the wives and the college boys off screen. It is a playful cinematic gesture, to be sure, akin to the closing shot of *I Was a Male War Bride*, but like many later Hawks comedies *The Cradle Snatchers* can be understood as an argument for taking playfulness seriously and responsibly. It is precisely the lack of that consciousness, in the comedies and elsewhere, that leads to disaster in Hawks.

Fig Leaves (1926)

Fig Leaves and *Paid to Love* bracket *The Cradle Snatchers* chronologically and can both be seen to share with it a like set of concerns and a similar narrative impulse. In *Fig Leaves*, however, roles are less reversed than foregrounded, though again the method for doing so involves a series of contrasting characters and situations.

The key situational contrast in *Fig Leaves* is generally characterized in simple terms as a matter of "then" and "now." Both Bogdanovich and Jeffrey Richards, for example, describe the film's structure as having two parts: "a Stone Age prologue and a main story set in the present" (Richards, 23). And both take Hawks at his word that the contrast signifies the fact "that people haven't changed much" (Bogdanovich, 7). But the film's structure is more complicated than that, both in its temporal aspects and in its significance—and that complexity is crucial for our understanding of the film's narrative action, which involves the marital mix-ups of Adam and Eve Smith. That is, the film's structural sophistication serves as a "lens" through which we view what is in some respects justly described as a melo-dramatic plot.

No serious attempt is made, for instance, to contrast history with prehistory. Rather, life in the prehistorical sequences is lived com-pletely in modern terms, even if the "technology" and the props involved—Adam's coconut and sand alarm clock, the tablet-of-stone newspaper ("Bad Blood between Cain and Abel"), the commuter train pulled by a dinosaur ("The 8:15")—are vaguely Edenic. Even "original sin" is recast into the modern idiom: eating the apple gave Eve "the gimmies," Adam complains, "first twin beds and now it's clothes"; and the snake is less a Satan figure, who tempts once and then leaves, than a next door neighbor ("Good morning, Eve") accus-tomed to dropping by for morning coffee.

Mise-en-scène and temporal disjunction, furthermore, also func-tion to qualify and comment on the film's "historical" dimension. Thus the general shape and layout of Adam and Eve's Garden of Eden cottage is identical in key aspects to that of their walk-up apartment in the modern sequences: door ways, furnishings, even wall decorations in both sets are placed and photographed so as to emphasize their identity. This identity is further underlined at film's end when Hawks cuts back and forth between the Garden of Eden and New York City—but without effecting any corresponding change in the film's action. Eve in the modern sequence has learned her lesson regarding the value of her marriage relative to her wardrobe, and she picks up a broom and prepares to chase her scheming, across-the-hall neighbor out the door of the Smith apartment. Dissolve, then, to Eden, where the broom-wielding Eve chases the neighborly snake out the door of the cottage while Adam (as in the modern sequence) waits outside the door to see what will happen. Adam and Eve then come close to openly reconciling—at which point Eddie McSwiggen, a character from the modern sequence, shows up in cave-man regalia and urges Adam, once again, to show Eve who's boss. Adam, however, prefers theatricality to cave-man brutality and he does his half-hearted best to look stern. Soon, however, Adam's stern expression breaks down and he tells Eve that Cain and Abel are having a "slaying party"—would she like to go? Eve self-consciously protests that she hasn't "a thing to wear." Adam responds with a mock-swoon—at which point we cut back to the modern era as Eve "steadies" him; and then the

Foregrounding appearances: Adam (George O'Brien) and Eve (Olive Borden) in successive images from Fig Leaves.

film fades out as Adam and Eve smile self-consciously at each other and embrace.

It is not the case, then, that the temporal aspect of the film's structure, its alternation of past and present, functions to assert a "likeness" of two eras, as it does, say, in *Intolerance* (1916) where separate actions carry similar implications. It is rather that the action of the film is *continuous*, so that the alternation of eras (of sets and costumes, essentially) fulfills a double function: (1) it foregrounds the modern behavioral code, especially its sexual component (in that the stereotypical sex role expectations are so clearly inappropriate in the Edenic context); and (2) it underlines the arbitrariness of appearances by demonstrating how readily they can be changed while *not* changing the character of the action. All of which is crucial to our understanding of the film's plot for the issues of sexual role playing and social appearance are exactly those which are raised by the film's action.

Like *The Cradle Snatchers*, then, *Fig Leaves* is a film *about* acting, though the roles in *Fig Leaves* are more social than theatrical. Thus at the film's beginning the main characters, Adam and Eve, are concluding their honeymoon: they are just learning how to play the husband and wife roles. Furthermore, each of them is coached or pressured, Eve by the snake, by Alice Atkins, and by couturier Josef Andre, Adam by coworker Eddie McSwiggen, to play their respective sexual roles in superficial and largely negative terms. Thus Alice, herself quite a clothes-horse, tells Eve to "get all the pretty clothes [she] can regardless of Adam." Thus Andre purposefully sets out to seduce Eve away from Adam by showering her with romantic verbiage and elegant finery, attempting to make her one more statue in his collection of high fashion mannequins. And thus Eddie constantly encourages Adam to "disconnect [Eve] with a pipe wrench"—even offering to play the wife role so Adam can practice his cave-man tactics.

None of which is intended to describe *Fig Leaves* in primarily melodramatic terms. Even the "villains" in the film are portrayed playfully, especially the foppish Andre, who anticipates later Hawks characters like *Twentieth Century*'s Oscar Jaffe in his propensity—if not his capacity—for extravagant self-dramatization (Andre only has one seduction routine, we eventually discover, which he uses repeatedly). Furthermore, Adam and Eve are generally characterized by resiliency (coconuts bounce off Adam's head; Eve is unhurt when struck by Andre's car), by their flexibility (as evidenced by their broad physical gestures), and by their self-consciousness (Eve, for example, interrupts her hysterics to sneak a look at Adam)—so it seems unlikely that either will succumb completely or permanently to the advice or schemes of those around them. Neither does. Adam does have a drink with Alice and is amused at the thought that Eve should be jealous. But he eventually decides that Eve deserves a new coat and goes, fortunately as it turns out, to Andre's, where he sees Eve modeling a revealing evening gown. He is upset at her lack of respect, for him and for herself, and decides to leave her. But he comes back to their apartment almost as soon as Eve finds his farewell note—at which point he sees Eve chase Alice out with the broom. Eve, likewise, while she yearns for new clothes and works as a model to earn them, never takes Andre seriously as a rival to Adam. Indeed, when she sees past his romantic facade and discovers his real intentions she plants a kick on the seat of his pants. And she doesn't believe it for a minute when Alice tells her that Adam gave her the new coat she is wearing. The melodrama in the film is more a matter of appearances than reality, appearances which Adam and Eve eventually see through, and it is limited to a few moments toward the end of the film—and even those moments of concern are qualified by the film's general quality of playfulness and good humor. Indeed, the extent to which the playful self-consciousness of the film parallels and in some sense guarantees that of the main characters is reinforced in the film's final moments: the flash back to Eden is simultaneous with Eve's decision to chase Alice out of the apartment, as if character action and the "action" of the film surface itself were each in some sense a function of the other.

Role "reversal" is thus a very minor element in *Fig Leaves*. But the more general issue of role playing or role testing is central to the movie. At the beginning of *Fig Leaves* Adam and Eve are marital neophytes and through the course of the film's action they "try out" various marital roles—the deceitful wife, the stern husband—only to realize that those socially dictated roles are destructive of the trust, the respect, and the self-awareness which form the foundation of their relationship. Thus at film's end both are seen to reject either the person or the advice of characters who have hitherto influenced them. The film therefore confirms the viability of marital roles, but the viability of the Adam/Eve match is essentially a private matter, depending more upon the intelligence and the commitment of the characters involved than upon the institution of marriage itself. In that respect, at least, *Fig Leaves* is remarkably typical of Hawks, looking forward particularly to films like *His Girl Friday* and *Monkey*

Business where marital relationships and roles are put to the test of human experience. And it is precisely this ability to keep social roles and personal realities appropriately balanced that *Fig Leaves* serves to celebrate, both in its mise-en-scène and its action.

Paid to Love (1927)

The social conventions foregrounded or reversed in *Paid to Love,* like those in *Fig Leaves* and *Cradle Snatchers,* are primarily matters of class and sex (both issues are implicit in the title); and despite its often slapstick tone and its comic-opera setting, the overall movement of *Paid to Love* is consistent with the earlier comedies in demonstrating the human consequences of taking conventionality too much for granted or too readily at face value. Indeed, the central intrigue of the film—which involves importing a Parisian actress to the kingdom of San Savona to arouse the sexual interest of the crown prince—reflects the issue of conventionality in several of its aspects.

The impetus for the scheme, to begin with, involves the financial health of the realm; the American financier who comes to advise the king refuses to grant a loan until the issue of Prince Michael's sexual preference is settled. As the financier puts it: "The prince that doesn't consider marriage might be unpopular—risky security for our loan." But the prince's sexuality is *not* really at issue, despite the king's conviction that Michael's only interest is motorcars. It is not that Michael is uninterested in women. He is attracted to Dolores (the actress) the very moment he sees her, and with no prompting whatsoever on her part. Indeed, she is unconscious at the time. It is rather the case that Michael is not interested in the women his father provides. Hence the fact that Michael (successfully) hides his identity from Dolores; he seems to understand, however intuitively, that social roles and sexual integrity can often be at odds and Michael quite properly sets a higher priority on sexual honesty. Indeed, his greatest sin in the film is not a lack of sexuality (as most critics seem mistakenly to assume) but a lack of sexual trust—a lack which threatens to destroy his relationship with Dolores.

The film's general thematic thus involves a conflict between social/ sexual roles and personal needs; but the film also falls fairly clearly into three sections (in this it recalls *Cradle Snatchers*), each of which approaches the general issue in fairly specific terms. The film's first section, for example, is devoted primarily to initiating the central intrigue, to hatching the plot and casting the parts, and it is played largely for slapstick, especially to the degree that the various gags serve to puncture or at least to foreground various sorts of social or sexual conventions. Two such gags or gag sequences are well worth noting.

For example, the film opens (after a brief scene at the palace) with the financier pacing up and down beside his stalled limousine while his moustachioed driver (a James Finlayson look-alike) tries unsuccessfully to restart the vehicle. Soon thereafter an elegant touring car pulls up and the financier pleads his position (he has to get to the palace) and asks for a ride—only to be turned down by Michael's philandering royal cousin Eric (William Powell), who is too busy with his back-seat paramour to give Roberts (the financier) a lift. Fortunately for San Savona, the crown prince is also out driving—and he stops to see if he can help. Rather than ask for a lift, however, Roberts glances at Michael's overalls, declares that the prince looks "dirty enough to be a mechanic," and asks Michael to look at the motor. Michael promptly and gladly fixes the car; Roberts does a doubletake and hands him a "real American dollar," urging him to go buy a title with it; and the gag's payoff comes in the following scene at the palace when Michael shows up and gently deflates the financier's self-importance by giving him back his coin under cover of a handshake. The overall point of the sequence is fairly evident: the appearance of wealth is no guarantee of worth or position. Put another way, it is already clear that Michael's open-faced concern for others is to be preferred to his cousin's variety of sexual self-indulgence, which involves switching paramours as readily as he changes uniforms (we never see his first girl again.)

The second noteworthy gag sequence from the first part of *Paid to Love* takes place in Paris at the "Café des Apaches" and serves primarily to introduce Dolores, though here too issues of sexuality and theatricality are central. More specifically, Dolores can be seen as the prototypical Hawksian female, independent of spirit and self-assertive in her gestures: for the first time we see the cigarette-play which becomes associated in Hawks with the development of human relations (Dolores takes a cigarette from the king's hand—and will later take one from Michael's) and we also see an early instance of that characteristic hands-on-hips gesture by means of which Hawksian characters "claim" their space (as Dolores claims the dance floor of the café).

Such gestures are also to be seen, however, as part of Dolores's "act." That is, like many a Hawksian female (like Bonnie in *Only*

Angels or Slim in *To Have and Have Not*), Dolores survives in a male-dominant society by becoming an entertainer of sorts. And Dolores's "acting" raises two issues in its immediate context. On the one hand the "lovers' quarrel," wherein Dolores "stabs" her paramour offstage and then dumps his catsup-smeared "corpse" across a café table, is played to the melodramatic hilt, not only in its props and gestures (the dagger in the garter, Dolores blowing cigarette smoke out the side of her mouth) but also in its editing (Hawks cuts repeatedly between "backstage" and "onstage") and its framing (gauzy "devil woman" close-ups à la Sternberg, for example). The whole charade (especially from our perspective) is hilariously overblown; so much so that even Roberts finally catches on to the gag and decides that Dolores is the girl to bring Michael to his senses—all of which implies that theatricality, when it is undertaken self-consciously and in good spirits, represents a form of emotional honesty.

On the other hand, however, there is a sense in which Dolores's "act" carries negative implications as well. At the beginning of the sequence she is backstage reading a book, and when the time comes to go on she remarks to her partner: "Come on, Pierre, time to go to work—one must eat." And the café sequence concludes, after Dolores accepts the job offered by Roberts, on a tight medium shot of Dolores, a quizzical, almost melancholy expression on her face. Thus, despite the fact that she throws herself into the immediacy of her Apache dancer role with real enthusiasm, it is clearly the case that Dolores longs to escape the circumstances which make playing the "devil woman" role her only means of survival. Hence, on the one hand, her willingness to take the job; and hence, on the other, her willingness to fall in love with Michael—both represent opportunities to escape the ersatz passion of the Apache dive, though the latter, clearly, is the one she (and Hawks) most value.

The tone of the film's second section becomes increasingly serious as the "plot" hatched by Roberts and the king becomes increasingly unraveled and beyond their control—despite their naive conviction that everything is going according to plan. Which is not to say (as Jean Gili implies) that the film becomes thereby less comic (92–93). It is rather the case that the "chance" occurrences which undermine the scheme hatched by Roberts and the king eventually require everyone (with the exception of Eric) to come to a deeper awareness of themselves and their roles, an awareness which ultimately liberates them from the more negative aspects of the social/sexual parts which they play at the film's beginning.

Two such "chance occurrences" are crucial to the direction taken by the film's action in its second section and both plot lines, once initiated, involve the problematic relationship between social roles and personal needs. The earlier coincidence of the two involves the previously mentioned first meeting of Michael and Dolores. She is on her way to San Savona, her car runs out of gas, and she stumbles through a driving rain toward the lighted windows of Michael's seaside house. The storm, however, is not to be read negatively. Rather, like many such storms in Hawks, it is to be seen as carrying positive connotations in its association of darkness, water, and a cleansing sexual honesty. Specifically, Dolores is so exhausted by the time she gets to the door that she collapses. Thus neither she nor Michael has opportunity to play roles until after the immediate issue of her physical welfare is settled. If anything, Michael's taking care of Dolores enforces sexual honesty on both of them: he undresses her (we do not see the action—only her clothing hung up to dry) and she is delighted by the innocent pleasure he obviously took doing it. Indeed, after the awkward Michael takes a slapstick tumble, tripping backward over her lingerie, Dolores gets up and looks at herself in a full-length mirror, as if trying to see herself anew, through Michael's eyes. It's only at the end of the scene, when she (apparently) thinks about her mission, that the smile fades from her face. The rainstorm and empty gas tank thus provide Michael and Dolores with an opportunity to be honestly themselves, but neither feels capable of being his or her private self for long without disguising or denying the public self, he as Prince, she as a cabaret dancer—and the danger implicit in this public/private split is clarified by the actions of Michael's royal cousin Eric.

After her interlude at Michael's seaside villa, Dolores continues on to San Savona and upon arriving receives instructions by phone from Roberts—at which point "chance" intrudes a second time. Unbeknownst to Roberts, his entire conversation, including his plans for the rendezvous between Michael and Dolores, is overheard by Eric, who just happens to be sitting in a high-backed chair in another part of the room. Predictably enough, Eric seizes the opportunity and arranges to take Michael's place at the rendezvous—and Dolores is deceived because Roberts had described Michael to her in only the most general social terms, in terms of time and place (a corner table,

Prince Eric (William Powell) and Dolores (Virginia Valli) role-playing in Paid to
Love.

three o'clock) and in terms of external appearance (his white military uniform). As things turn out it *is* an accurate description of Eric—who can be seen as Michael's opposite: where Michael is dissatisfied with his public role, Eric is completely identified with his. On several occasions, for example, Eric almost literally becomes part of the upper-class decor, in the king's office, as we have seen, and in Dolores's elegant bedroom, where Eric sits unnoticed in a corner while Dolores begins to undress. More importantly, Eric sees human relations almost completely in classbound terms, with nothing but the most superficial regard for personal realities. The closest he comes to Dolores is to sniff, however gracefully, her lingerie. And when Dolores catches him in her bedroom and orders him out, he responds in clear-cut class terms. He was under the impression, he tells her, that she "was hired to amuse the royal household"; and, upon seeing the prince's ring upon her hand, he seizes it, assuring her that "A prince may play but he doesn't marry his plaything, particularly a commoner." Indeed, Eric's gestures and attitudes are so self-contained as to smack of autoeroticism: hence the fact, perhaps, that he is frequently seen eating. While watching Dolores undress, for example, he slowly peels a very phallic banana and proceeds to consume it as Dolores puts on her robe.

The danger faced by Michael and Dolores in part two of the film thus involves the tendency, embodied by Eric, to let social roles or appearances define or delimit personal realities. Indeed, when Michael confronts Dolores with his ring, both of them momentarily fall into that trap. She admits that she had been "paid to love" him, at which point he forces himself upon her (he "breaks" her string of pearls); he then begs her forgiveness and she replies that she should have expected it—as if Michael were no different from Eric, as if she were nothing but a "plaything." And in some sense both deserve the comeuppance they get—not only because they act so badly when they finally confront one another, but because neither is trusting enough or self-possessed enough to be completely honest and open. Put another way, in maintaining such rigid distinctions between their private and public selves both Michael and Dolores effectively accept and internalize exactly those conventions of behavior embodied by Eric—however much they may despise themselves for doing it.

The film's third and final section, accordingly, is concerned to reassert that sense of self-aware playfulness demonstrated by Michael and Dolores in the film's opening scenes—but now against the background provided by part two. Again Roberts threatens to withhold funds from San Savona if the king fails to insure the sexual happiness of the prince. But this time the motive is less an abstract desire for financial stability than it is an immediate sense of remorse and personal concern; and likewise the means are less a matter of deception than collaboration. Rather than be bound by convention, Roberts and the king, with Michael's full knowledge and approval, agree to play with convention: if Michael can't marry a commoner they'll just go right ahead and make Dolores a duchess. As Roberts puts it—"she'll be the first duchess in history without a double chin." Thus the film's final scene takes place back at the Café des Apaches, an appropriately theatrical context for the "role reversal" which takes place when Michael, Roberts, and the king interrupt Dolores's act, Michael to beg forgiveness once again, Roberts and the king to make amends for their earlier cruelty. And "role reversal" works both ways. Michael offers to make Dolores a part of his "act"; and by so doing he effectively becomes part of hers. Indeed, as they embrace, a café patron comments: "That's just an act—they do it every night."

When seen in holistic terms, then, it must be said that the values celebrated in *Paid to Love* are thus quite consistent with those celebrated in the other two silent comedies and in Hawks's comic films generally: in nearly every case we see people suffer under the strain of social roles or expectations, and in most instances those roles are either reversed or loosened up by recourse to more role-conscious if not positively theatrical modes of behavior. In stylistic terms, furthermore, the silent comedies, like most of the later ones, invoke a double perspective: the self-consciousness of the characters within the film is reinforced by the self-consciousness *of* the film itself. In *Fig Leaves* and *Cradle Snatchers* this "doubling" is evidenced primarily by outright manipulation of the film surface, by means of flashbacks, obviously artificial sets, or jump cuts. *Paid to Love* evidences a similar double perspective—but the "cinematic" element is provided less by photographic manipulation (though under this heading one could quite properly discuss the film's occasional and essentially mimetic tracking shots) than by a self-conscious invocation of specific generic conventions. We see this in the earlier films, too. Both *Fig Leaves* and *Cradle Snatchers*, for example, recall to mind the De Mille of *Adam's Rib* (1923) and *Don't Change Your Husband* (1919) and the Keaton of *The Three Ages* (1923) and *College* (1927). But in *Paid to Love* generic citation becomes a major component of the aesthetic whole. More specifically, *Paid to Love* can be read as an extended homage to and critique of Von Stroheim's *Foolish*

Wives (1922) and *The Merry Widow* (1925). Thus Roberts in *Paid to Love* recalls the American envoy in *Foolish Wives*: both are on missions to a Mediterranean principality. And *Foolish Wives* also features a storm sequence similar to that in which Dolores in *Paid to Love* seeks shelter at Michael's seaside villa. More centrally, the sexual triangle in *Paid to Love* recalls that in Von Stroheim's version of *The Merry Widow*: in both films a working-class female dancer is courted by an idealistic crown prince and his more cynical royal cousin, and in both films the crown prince (and the cousin, too, in Von Stroheim) pretends to be nothing more than an army officer. Von Stroheim's vision is the more cynical, in that social pressures or entanglements pose a far greater threat to human relationships in *The Merry Widow* than they do in *Paid to Love*—and that is the essential point. Conventions, both cinematic and social, are generally loose enough to be "played with" in Hawks, though not in Von Stroheim, and it is that quality of playfulness—in *Paid to Love* and elsewhere—which makes Hawksian comedy so vital a cinematic genre.

Sexuality and Rigidity—*A Girl in Every Port* (1928)

Implicit in the notion of Hawksian role reversal as critics usually frame and express it is a strong element of misogyny. It is generally women who initiate the reversals—or so the standard view has it—and by so doing such women assume power over their men, who, therefore, find themselves playing, quite literally in some instances, the "female" role. The positive alternative, according to the accepted picture of Hawks, is the exclusive, all-male group of the adventure films, which women threaten by their presence, and to which they gain entrance only by accepting masculine values. I have already suggested that this view of sexual relations in Hawks is grossly exaggerated and essentially inaccurate. And nowhere, perhaps, is this inaccuracy more damaging than in the case of *A Girl in Every Port* (1928), the one silent film which critics most often cite to support the contention that the basic Hawksian fable is one of male comradeship and female duplicity.

It is frequently observed that *A Girl in Every Port* seems to be two different films, the first a simple comedy of male camaraderie and fisticuffs, the second a triangle of confused personal/sexual loyalties, and one's "reading" of the film's implications depends upon how the relationship between the two "movements" is construed.[6] For most

critics the relationship is fairly simple and accords completely with
the standard view of the adventure films. Spike (Victor McLaglen)
and Bill (Robert Armstrong) are shipmates whose "beautiful male
friendship" (Haskell, 35) is threatened by a gold-digging circus per-
former (Louise Brooks) who "fleeces Spike of his savings and tries to
seduce Bill" (Richards, 26). Her actions set the two men at odds, in
that Spike believes himself betrayed by Bill, and the film concludes
when the two pals resolve their differences and swear that nothing
will ever come between them again. But to read the film in these
terms—as if the restoration of the relationship between Spike and
Bill genuinely resolves the film's major issues—requires one to ignore all which makes *A Girl in Every Port* both cinematically interesting and thematically typical of the bleaker strain of Hawksian adventure film. Put another way, the disturbing psychological implications
in *A Girl in Every Port* look forward less to the positive fables of male
teamwork such as *Only Angels Have Wings* and *Air Force* than to the
often negative fables of psychic obsession such as *Scarface, Tiger
Shark,* and *Land of the Pharaohs* (1955).

The issue of obsession is raised early in the film and colors the
relationship between Spike and Bill long before that relationship is
challenged by the presence of the Louise Brooks character. The film
opens as ship's mate Spike orders a sailor aloft to put on more sail:
Spike has a date "with a dame in Holland." Upon arriving in port
Spike checks his little black book, wherein he keeps a detailed record
of his previous conquests. The girl in this port, however, is by now
the mother of three children and Spike quickly shifts attention to
another Dutch girl whose availability is indicated by the fact that she's
riding a bicycle built for two. Spike climbs aboard; they cycle out into
the country; but Spike rejects her otherwise welcomed and recipro-
cated advances as soon as he sees a heart-and-anchor design on a
bracelet she wears. The swab (Bill, it turns out) whose mark it is has
been "beating [Spike's] time" in the last five ports. As Spike puts it:
"I'm tired of finding his heart and anchor mark on my women." The
point is fairly clear. Sexuality for Spike is defined primarily if not
exclusively in terms of an adolescent sort of male gamesmanship. He
literally keeps score and is so upset by getting "beat" that he loses all
sexual interest, despite the fact that the girl in question is very overtly
and openly interested in him. She hardly seems to matter.

The dangerous aspect of this kind of sexuality is clarified in the next
port—Rio de Janeiro. Again Spike finds that the first girl he eyes is
already attached. And the second girl, like the second girl in the

initial sequence, also sports a heart-and-anchor charm, though on her garter rather than her bracelet. But Spike's discovery is prefaced by a "showdown" scene in the cantina where the girl, "Maria," works. When Spike first enters, Maria is sitting at a table with a gaucho. She is extremely sensual, both in her leg-displaying posture and in her dress; and she is aggressively independent in her actions and gestures as well (she smokes a cigar, and jumps into Spike's arms as soon as she sees him in the doorway). No sooner do she and Spike embrace, however, than Maria's Brazilian paramour gets up from the table to confront Spike. Spike reaches behind his back for a bottle; but when he sees that the odds are four to one he puts the weapon down and walks out. Maria is very angry and stomps hands-on-hips to her bedroom—where she finds Spike emerging from the shadows. Again, they embrace with genuine enthusiasm; but when Spike slides his hand up her thigh he finds the heart-and-anchor charm—at which point he literally "drops" her, onto her bed, and stomps out in an angry and absentminded huff, right into the cantina, where he again confronts the gaucho and his cohorts. Knives fly. One strikes the door frame right next to Spike's head. And Spike has to run for his life. Again, the point is clear: Spike's obsessive desire to win the sexual race with his as-yet-unknown opponent is quite literally a threat to his life, particularly given the fact that all the other men in the world he inhabits play the same game by the same rules.

Spike finally catches up with Bill in the third port he visits—and their meeting is significant in several respects. To begin with, their initial meeting and its immediate consequences clarify the relationship between sexual gamesmanship and physical danger. Spike has entered another sailors' café and, as he approaches an oriental girl, a sailor seated at a nearby table sticks out a foot to trip him. Spike regains his balance and composure, asks the girl to dance, is turned down—at which point the sailor who had tripped him (Bill, it turns out) grins broadly, apparently quite pleased at Spike's discomfiture. As if in response to Bill's goading, Spike sets his sights on the next girl to enter the café, who promptly walks right past the eager Spike and sits down at Bill's table, while Bill, rubbing it in for all he's worth, deliberately and insultingly turns his back on Spike. It is more than Spike can take. He confronts Bill. Bill gets up, gestures innocently, and under cover of the gesture sneaks in the first punch. Waiters rush to grab Spike, but before he can return the blow the police show up. Both sailors share a disregard for cops (another obsession) and they declare a momentary truce with each other so that they can turn their

Sexual enthusiasm: Victor McLaglen as Spike in A Girl in Every Port.

attention to fighting the gendarmes. Throughout the scene Hawks maintains a balance of brutality and humor, the brutality associated largely with Bill's completely uncalled for behavior toward Spike, the humor existing largely in Hawks's treatment of the brawl which develops: the action is shot in fast motion and Hawks cuts repeatedly to a dance band which never stops playing (another form of obsession?). Even the humor, however, is such as to call the fisticuffs into question. What was only half-funny to begin with soon becomes both ridiculous and dangerous, and the effect is underlined when Hawks cuts to an extreme down shot taken from high above the brawl just as Spike and Bill are overwhelmed by the police.

The "obsessive" quality of the behavior of Spike and Bill is thus well established at the very beginning of their relationship. What is less clear at this point in the film is the matter of motivation, particularly in light of the fact that Bill suddenly loses interest in women as soon as he and Spike become shipmates. In retrospect, however, one can see that Bill's motives, and by analogy Spike's, are fairly clear and are explicated chiefly by iconography and gesture. To put it briefly, Bill is constantly associated with things lacking or broken or scarred, and his actions—his series of sexual conquests, his attempts to maintain his relationship with Spike—can be seen as attempts to compensate. There is no indication that Bill is homosexually interested in Spike; but keeping "Spike" around is a way of denying his own genuine lack of stature (he is very short) and his implied lack of sexual potency. Thus during their first brawl Bill is quick to grab a police billy club which he wields throughout the fight (Spike fights barefisted); once in jail he asks Spike to pull his finger back into joint (as if Spike could make it "longer"); he needs financial help from Spike to make his bail and gain his freedom; after the two of them walk absentmindedly off a pier and into the drink, Bill has to borrow a cigarette from Spike (Bill's own are all soggy and broken); and at one point Bill literally puts a chip on his shoulder, both to increase his height and to induce a brawl that will prevent Spike from making time with a woman.

It can hardly be said of the Spike/Bill relationship, then, that it represents an essentially healthy and adult kind of male comradeship of the sort seen in films like *Air Force* and *Hatari!* Rather, the relationship in *A Girl in Every Port* is clearly marked as adolescent by its combination of physical aggressiveness, especially toward authority figures like policemen (Spike is constantly running into them even when he is not fighting), and sporadic sexual interest: sex for both Spike and Bill is less an end in itself than a means by which one can demonstrate masculinity. Furthermore, it is quite clearly the case that Spike at least, however subliminally, understands the stunted-ness implicit in his circumstances. His relationships with women are presented and experienced in very positive terms—until such time as he comes across the inevitable heart-and-anchor charm; and he is twice very closely associated with families and children. Indeed, in both cases there is a possibility that Spike is the father of the child (or one of the children), a possibility which he finds both moving and frightening. Indeed, it is immediately after the latter of these two "family" scenes that Spike begins to contemplate marriage and set-tling down.

At least in Spike's eyes, then, his relationship with "Mademoiselle Godiva," a circus high diver, represents a positive desire to escape from the recurrent pattern of events which largely dominates the film's action: Spike's interest in women is constantly frustrated by Bill, either in person or in absentia (via the heart-and-anchor charm). Put another way, Spike is "locked" into a social role which precludes emotional and/or sexual maturity; and he does his innocent if ineffec-tual Victor McLaglen best to change things for the better by taking on new roles, farmer and husband as opposed to sailor and shipmate.

Unfortunately, however, the sexual logic of his life catches up to him in the form of the Louise Brooks character. It is not the case, as critics usually describe it, that she consciously sets out to break up the otherwise admirable relationship of Spike and Bill. That relationship is problematic to begin with. It is rather the case that she is a *product* of sailor sexuality. Indeed, she had so loved Bill at one point that she still carries his heart-and-anchor mark tattooed upon her arm; but he had "ditched" her as he had ditched all the others: hence, on the one hand, her sexual cynicism vis-à-vis Spike and his money (in this she looks forward to Lotta II in *Come and Get It* [1936] and to Slim in *To Have and Have Not*) and hence, on the other, her attempts to seduce Bill, who reads her advances not as expressions of sexual integrity (which they are) but as attempts to come between himself and Spike. The sense that Tessie (Brooks) is to be seen as a projection into the world of those negative qualities inherent in the sexual gamesman-ship of Spike and Bill is further reinforced by iconography, most obviously in her heart-and-anchor tattoo, but also by her association with pooled water (she and Bill are equated by the fact that both are swimmers; Spike quite pointedly can't swim at all) and with cigarettes (Bill's are soggy when he pulls Spike from the drink; the water which

Tessie's high dive splashes all over Spike makes his cigarette soggy, too).

Ultimately, then, it must be said that Tessie is far less at fault in what takes place than Spike and Bill; and she represents no real alternative, positive or negative, to the sexlessness which typifies the relationship between the two men. The one she loves will not love her back; she can't love the one who loves her. So once again Spike's legitimate sexual urges—which carry the film's most positive associations—are thwarted by Bill and his heart-and-anchor mark. In which case the film's conclusion, wherein Bill and Spike pledge loyalty to one another, must be read ironically: for Spike and Bill it seems a positive move, but in the larger context of the film it must be read as a form of entrapment. Indeed, the final reconciliation takes place in a low-ceilinged underground bar, a setting which recalls the jail cells where they had been locked up earlier and which contrasts remarkably with the spatial freedom associated with the sea. The ominousness of the setting and its implications is indicated by the fact that it looks forward to settings in the final scenes of *Scarface* and *Land of the Pharaohs* where central characters find themselves trapped in settings which had originally been intended as fortresses or treasure houses. They are trapped, quite literally, in and by their own plans and values.

The typicality of *A Girl in Every Port* cannot be argued, therefore, in positive terms, as if it were an embryonic version of the later, more upbeat adventure films. It is more accurate to say, particularly in the context of the earlier comedies, that *A Girl in Every Port* presents an early version of the negative Hawksian fable in which social and sexual roles become so rigidly defined as to preclude the sort of comic inversions or reversals which usually enable Hawksian characters, even in films like *Red River* and *Red Line 7000*, to overcome a rigid dedication to their own plans, plans which seem inevitably in Hawks to involve a denial or perversion of human sexuality. Put another way, misogyny in Hawks is not portrayed as a positive moral stance, as many critics assume. Just the contrary. Misogyny in Hawks is almost always correlated with characters—like Andre in *Fig Leaves* or Eric in *Paid to Love* or Bill in *A Girl in Every Port*—whose philandering is predicated on maintaining a particular and rigidly defined social role and expresses thereby a strong fear of the growth and change implicit in sexual relations. A brief look at one final Hawks silent, *Fazil*, will clarify the point.

Fazil (1928)

According to Jeffrey Richards, *Fazil*, among the silent films of Howard Hawks, is far and away the most "utterly untypical" film of an already atypical lot, "a complete but unashamed and uninhibited departure from characteristic terrain into realms of high romance" (26); and in this, Richards goes on, *Fazil* marks the "climax of Hawks' brief flirtation with the 'European Style'" which began with *Paid to Love* (27). We have already seen, however, the degree to which *Paid to Love* represents no real departure from the concerns and images which would come to typify the later Hawks—and the same can also be argued in reference to *Fazil*. Indeed, *Fazil* is especially interesting for the light it casts on other early films, like *A Girl in Every Port* and *Scarface* among several, which share a similar focus on the negative consequences which follow when characters become imprisoned by their own plans and values.

Like *Scarface*, *Fazil* begins and ends with death; and in both cases the executioner in the first instance is both killer and victim in the second. Thus Tony Camonte initiates the action of *Scarface* by rubbing out a rival mobster; at film's conclusion he effectively murders his sister when a police bullet glances off the steel plate which Tony is swinging shut (so that Tony's attempt to shut out the world is lethal to Cesca) and then he in turn is gunned down when he tries to make a mad break for it through police lines. Likewise, *Fazil* begins with the execution of a deserter; and its concluding sequence finds Fazil once again in pursuit, of his French-born wife, a pursuit which results in his own death (he is shot by a member of the European rescue party) and also in that of Fabienne (whom he poisons as they embrace).

Similar pairings of early and late shots or sequences are quite common in Hawks, both in the adventure films (e.g., *The Dawn Patrol, The Road to Glory* [1936], *Only Angels Have Wings*) and in the comedies (e.g., *Twentieth Century, Bringing Up Baby, Hatari!*), and it would be inaccurate to suggest that the implications are the same in every case. In the comedies, for example, such repetitions usually reflect upon "self-consciousness"—of the film as self-reflecting artifact and of the characters as self-aware personalities—and they help to measure the distance that the film has traveled. Thus *Monkey Business*, to take one instance, both begins and ends with Barnaby (Cary Grant) and Edwina (Ginger Rogers) Fulton preparing to go out, and in both instances they decide at the last minute to stay home. In the initial scene, however, their staying home results from

Barnaby's preoccupation with his research (he's trying to invent a youth-restoring drug): Barnaby can't quite seem to lock the door and turn out the house lights in proper sequence so Edwina decides they should stay in for the evening. In the second scene, by contrast, it's Barnaby, now freed from his preoccupation, who suggests that they stay home, and not to avoid embarrassment but to express affection, of the very sort that Barnaby's earlier mania had tended to preclude. Repetition in this case betokens meaningful variation. However, in *The Dawn Patrol,* to take a second example, repetition is far less positive in its implications. Life in *The Dawn Patrol* is determined by an apparently endless and repetitive sequence of orders given, missions flown, and names erased from the duty roster. But clearly the most powerful sort of repetition in *The Dawn Patrol* involves those sequences wherein command is passed down—from Brand to Courtney and from Courtney to Scott—and the new commander gives his first orders. In both cases it is clear that being commander involves an almost debilitating responsibility for the lives of others (hence Brand's jubilation at being ordered to the rear and Courtney's displeasure at taking over the squadron); and in that respect the repetition is and remains negative, a consequence of a deplorable set of social circumstances wherein human activity is devoted primarily to killing. It is worth remarking, however, that in the second instance, upon which the film concludes, the assumption of command also involves a strong implication of forgiveness. In taking over from Courtney, after Courtney's suicide mission, Scott's bearing and attitude—as well as his announcement that Courtney's sacrifice has earned the unit a special commendation—evidences his appreciation of Courtney's position and actions, an acceptance of the fact that Courtney had to order Scott's unskilled younger brother into action.

Repetition in *Fazil,* as the comparison to *Scarface* indicates, is essentially of the negative sort, both in its causes and consequences. The key to the narrative logic of the film, for example, is the essentially negative relationship between culture and feeling. In the first scene culture is defined as a matter of Arabic law: "For desertion there is but one punishment—death." Thus Fazil shows no mercy for the deserter whose execution he orders. In the second scene, which introduces Fabienne, culture is defined by reference to courtship and marriage. Fabienne is, a title tells us, a "child of caprice—unfettered by custom or tradition"; and her response when asked whether she will ever marry indicates a genuine (and, in her case, prophetic) fear of the institution: "I am afraid of marriage, afraid of anything that might take away the freedom I love." The point to make, however, is that both Fazil and Fabienne are defined by their "relation" to culture; and the tragic quality of the film involves their inability— once they have met and married—to redefine their relation to society and to each other in terms which would permit the continued expression of the positive emotions which they never stop feeling for one another. Each will make some attempt at accommodation—Fabienne by following Fazil to Arabia, Fazil by dismissing (temporarily) his harem—but neither seems capable of abandoning the culturally determined views of sexual relationships which hinder them. Thus Fabienne "walks out" on Fazil on two occasions (while in Paris she quite pointedly leaves the room after disobeying Fazil's order to cancel a dinner engagement, and in Arabia she begs to be rescued) and Fazil repeats the pattern by walking out twice on his part (he leaves Paris when he finds himself unable to make concessions to Western manners and walks out of Fabienne's harem room when she questions him about the new wife he has taken).

We may characterize the theme of *Fazil*, then, as involving contrasting "visions" of sexual ethics. Indeed, the matter of who can see whom is central both to the action and imagery of the film. The courtship of Fazil and Fabienne is almost entirely a matter of exchanged glances; they first see each other Lubitsch-fashion across a Venetian canal, for example. And from the very first Fazil wants to keep Fabienne to himself so that "the eyes of other men" cannot see her. The danger implicit in such a single-minded view of sex is evidenced during the brief honeymoon sequence (which anticipates a similar sequence in *Monkey Business*—both Fazil and Barnaby Fulton have a go at high diving) when Fazil repeatedly takes his eyes off the road (or the lake) and his hands off the wheel of the vehicle he pilots (a car, a motorboat) in order to embrace Fabienne. When the conflict comes to a head, furthermore, after the honeymoon, it comes over the issue of sight: shall Fazil's Arab servant "look upon" Fabienne's face and shall Fabienne continue to "see" John Clavering, a previous suitor and friend, socially?

Finally, there is the specific issue of Fazil's gaze, of his eyes, which is connected by association with his inability to express his feelings in words (a frequent failing of Hawksian males). From the very beginning of their relationship Fabienne expresses her fear of Fazil's eyes, a fear based on her inability to understand the nature of his feelings for her: "Your eyes—they frighten me—I do not understand them." And repeatedly she tries to come to terms with Fazil and her own fears by ritualistically kissing his eyes, first one, then the other, as if hoping that emotion itself could override the social pressures which force Fazil to see her and treat her as he does. Such kisses are frequently accompanied by requests on Fabienne's part that Fazil speak "the words" he has "never said"—and it is only in their final embrace, after Fazil is shot and after he administers the poison to Fabienne, that he can openly acknowledge his feelings. Indeed, his final action is to close her lifeless eyes and kiss them tenderly, as if, by repeating her gesture, to acknowledge his own blindness and culpability, his prior inability to see her apart from the Arab context and culture. (This equation of psychic rigidity and blindness, it should be noted, is a recurrent Hawks motif: see *Scarface, Today We Live* [1933], *Road to Glory, Only Angels Have Wings,* and *Rio Bravo.*)

Like *A Girl in Every Port,* then, *Fazil* can best be understood as an argument *against* allowing social or psychological pressures to encourage the denial of genuine sexual commitments. In each case the central male character (Spike, Fazil) evidences a genuinely passionate and positive interest in sexuality—Spike in the early scenes of *A Girl in Every Port,* before he meets Bill; Fazil in his relationship with Fabienne—and in both cases the alternative is either some form of philandering (having "a girl in every port," keeping a harem) or rejection (Spike walks out on Tessie, Fazil walks out on Fabienne). The two films are different largely to the extent (1) that social pressures in *A Girl in Every Port* are more clearly personified, in the character of Bill, than they are in *Fazil,* where the social codes have been internalized by the central characters; and (2) that the negative consequences of allowing social codes to determine personal and especially sexual conduct are far more clearly imaged in the double murder that concludes *Fazil.* One would be hard pressed to describe either film as a comedy. And to that extent neither is really typical of the mature Hawks. But both films look forward to the Hawks of the early 1930s, the Hawks of *The Dawn Patrol, The Criminal Code, Tiger Shark,* etc., and as such neither film can be written off as atypical or uninteresting.

4

The Father and the Law

I HAVE ARGUED THUS FAR that the Hawksian world view is on the whole a comic one regardless of genre, focusing on the ability of Hawksian characters in both the comedies and the adventure films to trust to nature and to each other and thereby to give up defensive or oppressive social and sexual roles. And yet, as my discussions of *A Girl in Every Port* and *Fazil* indicate, there are certain films in the canon—most of them produced in the late 1920s and early 1930s—which do not seem to fit comfortably under this comic rubric. Such movies are still recognizably Hawksian. Indeed, for most critics it is films like *The Dawn Patrol* and *Scarface* which most thoroughly epitomize the essentially tragic quality of the Hawksian cosmos in general. I believe it demonstrable, however, that even the more tragic of Hawks's films are not well accounted for by the standard view of the Hawksian cinema; and furthermore, when properly understood, such films can be seen to enrich our appreciation of the more overtly comic films in the canon, to enrich our sense of the *resonance* of those films, by demonstrating the ethical necessity of adopting a more comic, a more *social* view of experience. Indeed, it is precisely for rejecting—or for being forced to reject—a comic view of experience that characters often come to grief in the Hawks films of the early 1930s.

A common feature of comic plots generally is some sort of sexual triangle involving a young man, a young woman, and an authority figure who stands in dramatic and thematic opposition to their union. Often the authority figure is a father—to the young man (as in Plautus) or to the young woman (as in Shakespeare)—in which case the triangle recalls and resonates to the Oedipus myth. In other instances the rival is not a father but a father surrogate, either in age (a *miles gloriosus*) or by virtue of the surrogate's close association with the established social and legal order (the various Prince or Duke figures in Shakespeare, for example): again the rival or obstacle represents a principle of authority and stasis while the young couple represents the principles of sexual growth and social change. Of course, such character/plot patterns by themselves are not exclusive to comedy—*Oedipus Rex* is the prototypical tragedy, after all—which tells us that comedy and tragedy may resonate alike to the same or similar mythic implications. But the comic movement is generally toward *integration*. The young lovers overcome the opposition to their match and the *senex* or "blocking figure" often undergoes a change of heart which allows him to participate in the comic festivities with which such works often conclude. In tragedy, on the other hand, the essential movement is toward *disintegration*: central characters suffer death (Lear) or exile (Oedipus) and the focus falls more on loss than on gain. Note, then, that certain comic characters, in Shakespeare for instance, are *not* integrated (Malvolio in *Twelfth Night*, Shylock in *The Merchant of Venice*) or are integrated almost despite their behavior or deserts (Angelo in *Measure for Measure*). And comic works which focus strongly on such "blocking characters" often verge on tragedy, in tone if not in plot.

The Criminal Code (1931)

A number of early Hawks adventure films can be read as "tragic comedies" of the *Merchant of Venice* sort. Oedipal triangles appear frequently, for example, and in many cases serve to demonstrate the often problematic relationship in Hawks between legal or social power on the one hand and sexual growth and change on the other. *The Criminal Code*, for instance, features a father/daughter relationship which is challenged when the Constance Cummings character falls in love with convicted-murderer Robert Graham (Phillips Holmes). As district attorney, Walter Huston had prosecuted the boy out of questionable motives. The victim in Graham's case was the son of a wealthy father who controlled the newspapers; Brady (Huston) was up for reelection; so he threw the book at the boy even though fully aware of Graham's essential innocence and of the arbitrariness of "The Criminal Code." Brady even boasts that if he were the boy's lawyer he could "get him off." But Brady immediately turns around and promises the press "a quick conviction."

Later in the film, then, as prison warden, Brady once again faces a choice: he can allow the prosecution of Graham (for refusing to squeal on a fellow inmate wanted for murder) or he can parole the boy, though only at the risk of his own career. He makes the latter choice, partly to assuage his own guilt for his earlier transgression (he even chides the local state's attorney for upholding the same "eye for an eye" view of the law which he himself had championed earlier in the film), but the deciding factor in his choosing to let Graham go and "see him through" is his discovery of the relationship between Graham and his daughter ("I guess that's one thing the law doesn't cover").

Why that discovery should finally make him admit to the insufficiency of his previously inflexible devotion to "the law" is not explicitly stated. But it clearly involves an acknowledgment of youthful sexuality as a powerful and positive force. At the film's beginning Huston initiates his interrogation of Graham's street-walker girl friend by telling her to pull down her skirt ("the shade"); and his relationship to his daughter, Mary, is presented almost as that of husband to wife (they are often framed together in tight two shots). It's as if Brady's devotion to the law were a cover for, a way of denying, his own questionable or threatened sexuality. But the necessity or utility of that cover story falls apart when his daughter reveals her sexual feelings for Graham. To maintain *any* relationship with Mary he *must* side with Graham. Thus, despite the film's essentially comic conclusion—the reunion of Graham and Mary in her father's office— the emotional focus of the film and of the final scene is on Brady, the "blocking figure." Indeed, the film's closing image is of Brady isolated in close-up, looking disconsolately at his unlit cigar while Mary and Graham embrace offscreen.

Tiger Shark (1932)

Tiger Shark and *Barbary Coast*, the two films that Hawks made with Edward G. Robinson, can be seen as variations on the pattern established by *The Criminal Code*. The Robinson character in *Tiger Shark* (1932), like Huston's Brady in *Criminal Code*, is an authority figure, the captain of a tuna boat, whose personality is defined by reference to some sort of implicitly sexual lack (Brady lacks a wife, Mike Mascarenhas lacks a hand), and also by his strict adherence to "the law"—in *Tiger Shark* the marital code upon which Mike relies to guarantee his openly loveless marriage. The associative relationship is clear. In both cases adherence to "the law" functions psychologically as protection against sexual insecurity. Both men are involved in implicitly incestuous father/daughter relationships—Brady with his own daughter, Mike with the daughter of a deceased crew member—and both men are called into question when a younger man earns the love of "the daughter."

The chief difference between *The Criminal Code* and *Tiger Shark*, then, is that Brady in the earlier film is capable of letting go, of both Mary and the law, before it is too late; while Mike in *Tiger Shark* is not. When he discovers the relationship between his best friend, Pipes (Richard Arlen), and his daughter/wife, Quita (Zita Johann), he insists upon playing the vengeful father, aligning himself (or so he would like to think) with the "law" of nature ("The sharks—they settle things"), only to discover that "natural law"—as is generally the case in comedy—sides with the young couple. Mike dumps the unconscious Pipes overboard, into a dinghy, which Mike then attempts to sink by harpooning it. In the process, however, Mike's leg gets caught in a line and he is pulled into the shark-infested waters.

The "ruthlessness" of the ending of *Tiger Shark*, therefore, should not be attributed to an essentially malevolent natural order (as Andrew Sarris has suggested).[1] Quita never pretends to love Mike, however much she cares for him, and she and Pipes do their level and very ethical best to avoid hurting Mike. Rather, the malevolence in the film follows largely from Mike's rigid inability to acknowledge the emotional validity of the relationship between Pipes and Quita. Indeed, it is loyalty too rigidly defined which cost Mike his hand in the first place (he throws a man to the sharks in a dispute over water rations just before their lifeboat is spotted by a rescue ship). Mike, like many a father figure in Hawks, tries too hard to order the world according to his own plans. Mike's hook, indeed, is a marvelous physical and visual image of his mental state: it is hard, twisted, and turns back upon itself. And human plans—as we have seen in *Only Angels Have Wings, I Was a Male War Bride*, and *The Criminal Code*—are by themselves no guarantee of success in Hawks, especially when they are predicated on the denial of sexual honesty and integrity.

Barbary Coast (1935)

Barbary Coast is a remarkably interesting film for several reasons. It is one of the most Sternbergian of Hawks films, for example, despite the fact that it was written by Ben Hecht and Charles MacArthur—rather than by Jules Furthman, with whom we normally associate the more romantic films of both Von Sternberg (*Morocco, Shanghai Express*) and Hawks (*Only Angels Have Wings, To Have and Have Not*). More important in the present context, however, is the degree to which *Barbary Coast* may be read as a later example of Hawksian tragi-comedy—though one in which the balance of tragedy and comedy can clearly be seen to shift.

Once again an Oedipal triangle is at film's center, again raising issues both sexual and social. The Edward G. Robinson character in *Barbary Coast*, Louis Chamalis, is quite explicitly *the* authority figure in the "mud puddle" that is gold-rush–era San Francisco. Through most of the film he controls the local authorities, especially the alcoholic local judge; and when Chamalis's authority is called into question by a newly founded newspaper he threatens to smash its printing press. As Chamalis puts it, over the protest of the newspaper's editor, "I am the law around here and I give the orders." Chamalis is also, though less directly, a "father figure" akin to those in *The Criminal Code* and *Tiger Shark*. He takes Mary Rutledge (Miriam Hopkins) under his wing when she arrives in San Francisco to find her mail-order fiancé dead, and the two strike a cynical bargain of convenience: he will give her shelter and position while she will attract customers to the crooked roulette wheel in his gambling den, the "Bella Donna" (this association of crooked gambling, drugs—belladonna—and sexual cynicism looks forward to *The Big Sleep*, where the Lauren Bacall character is named Vivian "Rutledge"). The Oedipal aspect of the Hopkins/Robinson relationship is clarified and reinforced by the entrance midway through the film of the Joel McCrea character, James Carmichael. Carmichael is a well-bred easterner who explains his presence in the gold fields by reference to his father. It was either work for his father or go find the golden fleece, as he puts it. And when Carmichael is fleeced of his gold at the crooked roulette wheel run by Hopkins he goes to work for Chamalis, who thus becomes both father (as employer) and rival (for Hopkins).

Barbary Coast may be said to differ from *The Criminal Code* and *Tiger Shark* in two important respects, both of which evidence a shift in Hawks toward a more positively comic view of experience. In both of the earlier two films, for example, the focus is clearly on the "father": in both cases it is this "blocking figure" whose values and actions are called into question, and both films conclude with a close-up of the older man (Brady looking off screen and then down in *Criminal Code*, the good hand of Mike Mascarenhas patting Pipes forgivingly on the back and then dropping lifeless in *Tiger Shark*). In

A Von Sternberg touch: Miriam Hopkins displays Marlene Dietrich-like cynicism in Barbary Coast.

Barbary Coast, by contrast, the focal character in the Oedipal triangle is no longer the older man but the "daughter." The film begins with the arrival in San Francisco of the Miriam Hopkins character; and the film concludes in a long shot of Hopkins as she runs to the ship that will carry her and Joel McCrea back to New York.

More importantly, it is the Hopkins character who is clearly at the film's moral and dramatic center. The key thematic issue in *Barbary Coast,* as in the earlier films, involves a conflict between sexual integrity on the one hand and self-interest too rigidly defined on the other—and that issue is personified by Hopkins at the outset. In the film's first scene she is the only passenger aboard ship who does not rejoice upon arrival in port, and her weariness is doubly significant. On the one hand her malaise is indicative of her motive for coming, to marry a wealthy prospector; but on the other it is also clear that her Dietrich-like cynicism, her studied refusal to see San Francisco as an opportunity to be "reborn in the new land," is expressive of her own deeper idealism: her disgust is self-directed and evidences a genuine desire for something better. It is arguable, indeed, that her willingness to go along with Chamalis's proposition is in itself the result of a desire for punishment (it is not her only option). Note, however, that even in agreeing to work for Robinson she begins to reassert the sexual integrity that her mail-order marriage had threatened: their relationship is framed almost exclusively in business terms, and she quite pointedly tells Chamalis that he'll need to learn to knock before he enters her bedroom.

The second aspect wherein *Barbary Coast* differs from *The Criminal Code* and *Tiger Shark* involves a sustained and strikingly Fordian concern with the concept and process of civilization. Both of the earlier films, to be sure, raise socially significant issues; and in *Tiger Shark*, at least, the Portugese community is presented in largely positive terms. But the society in *Barbary Coast*—like those which we see in later Hawks Westerns such as *Red River* and *Rio Bravo*—is a society in the making. Walter Brennan's Old Atrocity boasts, for instance, that there is a price on his head in every state in the union except California, and "they ain't organized yet." Such order as exists rests largely in the hands of Louis Chamalis; and he exercises that power solely for his own benefit. Indeed, there is a psychotic element to the exercise of Chamalis's influence. It is not enough, for example, to run a crooked roulette wheel: those who question his authority, however ineffectually, risk murder at the hands of Chamalis's inarticulate henchman—Knuckles. Furthermore, it is striking that Chamalis is only in full control of himself and his circumstances when he is within the walls of the Bella Donna. He extends his control outward by means of Knuckles and Old Atrocity; and when he does go out himself, even when accompanied, he tends to become enraged and lose control. It is only at film's end, when control of San Francisco has clearly passed into the hands of the citizenry, that Chamalis acquires a genuine measure of self-possession, ordering Mary to go back to Carmichael, and submitting, with real dignity, to his own arrest.

Standing in opposition to the rigid brutality of Chamalis's sort of "law and order" is a far more flexible and social kind of order: language. Three characters in particular are especially associated with language in *Barbary Coast*, and in each case language is presented as an explicitly positive and social force—as it is repeatedly in Hawks.

One such character I have already mentioned, James Carmichael. He is work-drunk (for the most part self-consciously so) from the moment he enters the film, and his words resonate to two sets of connotations. Carmichael's frequent references to Ulysses, for example, reflect his willingness to cut loose from the East (and his father) and venture westward. And he is also associated with the emotional integrity of the Romantic poets: he gives Mary a volume of Shelley, for instance, as a token of his regard. Another such character is Colonel Marcus Aurelius Cobb, drunkard, idealist, and Hechtian newpaper editor. He arrives aboard the same ship as Mary Rutledge and is determined to see his newspaper become "a beacon to guide the destiny" of San Francisco. (In this Cobb looks forward to and calls to mind the editor of *The Shinbone Star* in Ford's *The Man Who Shot Liberty Valance.*)

A third character associated with language in *Barbary Coast* is Jed Slocum. As acted by Ford stock-player Harry Carey, Slocum combines the qualities of Fordian dignity and Hawksian righteousness. He refuses, for example, to remove his hat when Chamalis's in-house judge turns the Bella Donna into a makeshift courtroom. But Slocum is also, and quite explicitly, a "spokesman" as well. He leads the group that swears out an arrest warrant for Knuckles after the latter murders Sandy Ferguson ("a warrant," as Chamalis puts it, "all printed out and everything"); and when the sheriff hesitates to serve and explain it, Slocum responds: "We'll do the talking." Furthermore, after Knuckles is "acquitted," it is Slocum who leads the group over to the newspaper office to enlist the aid of Colonel Cobb's *San Francisco Clarion.*

The essentially positive relationship in *Barbary Coast* between sexual and social integrity is evidenced repeatedly. When Chamalis orders Knuckles to smash Colonel Cobb's press, for instance, Mary intervenes on Cobb's behalf, thus saving the paper. It is the first "break" between Chamalis and Mary, the first time that she expresses overt disapproval of his actions, and Mary's kindness is effectively rewarded the next morning, when she gets caught out riding in another of those Hawksian rainstorms and takes refuge in a wayside cabin—where only moments earlier James Carmichael had likewise taken temporary shelter. Their meeting is thus fortuitous in the extreme; but, like many such chance occurrences in Hawks, it is associated through context and iconography with emotional and sexual integrity. Mary's integrity, her break with Chamalis, leads her to the meeting; and once inside the cabin she has the opportunity (like

Dolores in *Paid to Love*, for instance) to shed her cynical identity, both literally (she takes off her wet clothes) and figuratively (Carmichael does not know her as the "Swan" of the Bella Donna).

A similarly positive relationship between social and sexual integrity is also evidenced in the sequence of events leading to the film's conclusion. At one level, to be sure, Chamalis's downfall is attributable to public outrage, particularly after Knuckles finally murders Colonel Cobb. But Chamalis's vulnerability is largely a function of his almost frenetic desire to play the "father" role vis-à-vis Mary. While he sends most of his boys out to "set fire to San Francisco" Chamalis himself sets out in pursuit of Mary and Carmichael, both of whom willingly risk provoking Chamalis's anger for the sake of their relationship. Their exercise of sexual integrity is thus a contributing factor in the overthrow of Chamalis for drawing him out of the Bella Donna. So too, however, is Chamalis's own growing understanding of what their integrity implies. Though he phrases it in egotistical terms ("I don't take presents off anybody—I give 'em") Chamalis's decision to let Mary and Carmichael go represents an acknowledgment even on Chamalis's part that personal and emotional integrity are to be respected in others. Indeed, such respect is the very basis of a democratic society—a point which Hawks underlines in his mise-en-scène: no sooner does Chamalis tell Mary to return to the ship ("Don't you understand English—go on back to him") than the camera tracks backward from a tight two-shot of Chamalis and Mary to pick up Jed Slocum and his fellow vigilantes standing in the background of the frame.

It would be a mistake, in discussing *Barbary Coast*, to push the Ford comparison too far. There is nothing in Hawks quite like that characteristic concern with and respect for tradition which we find so often and so movingly in Ford. Such traditions as exist in Hawks, it is frequently observed, are largely ad hoc traditions, growing out of specific times and places and drawing their significance from their immediate human (social) context. In that respect, at least, Ford and Hawks are *not* alike. It is equally a mistake, however, to invoke the Ford/Hawks distinction as evidence that Hawks's adventure films are not strongly and in many respects positively concerned with the issue or concept of civilization.

Indeed, as I argued in regard to *Only Angels Have Wings*, the rejection of established society is often to be read negatively in Hawks, as the expression of egocentrism and immaturity. Jeff Carter, for instance, can be read as a benign version of Louis Chamalis: both are father figures (Jeff is often referred to as "Papa") and for both the exercise of authority involves a denial of sexual integrity (Jeff rejects Bonnie: Chamalis stands opposed to the union of Mary and Carmichael). No genuinely positive "society" can exist in such circumstances, it is clear, unless and until the rule of "the father" (or of the negative values he represents) can be broken, loosened up, or "reversed." That which needs to be rejected in Hawks is not, therefore, "society" in the abstract but rather specific social circumstances which are destructive of genuine social relationships. One such circumstance which is repeatedly undercut or condemned in Hawks is monopoly capitalism—as it is personified by characters such as Louis Chamalis in *Barbary Coast,* Barney Glasgow in *Come and Get It,* or Eddie Mars in *The Big Sleep*—hence the satiric strain in Hawks. That hardly makes Hawks a radical. But the implicit equation in Hawks of monopoly capitalism and emotional and social immaturity is striking nevertheless and constitutes a far more sophisticated view of society than Hawks is generally given credit for.

Scarface (1930)

Any act of criticism entails and depends upon an ability to categorize—to see a film working in one fashion rather than another. The validity of such a procedure is thus an empirical matter: do the proposed categories help or hinder our attempts to account for the data of the films? I have already suggested that the categories implicit in the standard view of Hawks are more reductive than illuminating. The present chapter, furthermore, effectively proposes a third category of Hawks film, a subset of the more general "adventure film" category, wherein strong father figures (or father surrogates) are called into question for attempting to assert their own vision of "the law" over and against both the common good and the sexual integrity of various "son" or "daughter" figures. Even within this subset, however, a further fine tuning is possible. That is, we may trace two different *versions* of this "tragedy of the father" fable. In one version the father figure actively seeks to acquire and exercise power; in the other the power is less sought than imposed, is less a goal than a burden. Among the former category, films like *The Criminal Code, The Crowd Roars,* and *Come and Get It* may be included; among the latter, films like *The Dawn Patrol, Viva Villa!* and *Ceiling Zero.* And the distinction is crucial for the light it throws on the problem of the Hawksian world view. The notion that the Hawksian universe is

The killer and the cross in Scarface.

basically hostile clearly does *not* work for films like *The Criminal Code, Barbary Coast,* and *Come and Get It* wherein the father figure clearly *earns* the fate which overtakes him. The world is less at fault in these instances than the characters. In films like *The Dawn Patrol,* however, there is very little direct sense of cause and effect. Characters suffer and die needlessly and senselessly. For such films the "hostile universe" hypothesis seems genuinely plausible. Discussing *Scarface* and *The Road to Glory* will help to clarify the distinction and also to specify more clearly the sources of hostility in the world of Howard Hawks.

It is often remarked that the basic metaphor in *Scarface* is the "X" or "cross" figure which appears repeatedly in the film's visuals, almost always in association with death. Thus in the film's opening sequence we watch Tony Camonte (Paul Muni) murder Big Louis—but what we see is Tony's shadow cast against a frosted glass panel, upon which also appears the pattern of a shadowy cross. The St. Valentine's Day massacre sequence, likewise, is "framed" by shots of the roof supports of the garage where the killings take place, supports which form

a pattern of interlocked "X" figures—distorted crosses. Just before
Tony guns down Gaffney (Boris Karloff) in the bowling alley, Gaffney
rolls a strike: cut to close-up as an "X" is marked on his scoresheet.
And when Tony kills Guino Rinaldo (George Raft)—not knowing that
Guino and Cesca (Tony's sister) are married—he does it in the doorway of the Rinaldo apartment, number ten ("X"). As Robin Wood has
it, however, the "cross" or "X" symbolism serves essentially to provide a point of moral reference in what might otherwise be seen as a
remarkably immoral movie. The horrific exploits of Tony Camonte
are presented as having a kind of manic and captivating intensity, an
intensity which Hawks then calls into question by means of the
repeated image of the cross, an image which Wood interprets in
essentially religious terms: hence the film's "particular flavor of pro-
fanity."[2] I would agree that the crosses in *Scarface* invoke religious associations; one flaw of the Hawks-as-existentialist position is
its almost complete inability to allow for the sincere (though not
doctrinaire) religiosity of films like *Today We Live, Road to Glory,*
and *Sergeant York.* But the "X" figure in *Scarface* also has other
resonances, beyond the religious ones, resonances which are equally
central to our understanding of the film.

One such resonance involves the abstract "shape" of the film's plot
structure. *Scarface,* that is, has two plots, two narrative chains of
actions and motives, both essentially Oedipal in configuration, each
of which runs implicitly counter to the other: the two plots together
may be thought of as forming an "X." The first such plot—which
dominates the first three-quarters of the film—involves the rise to
power of Tony Camonte. He begins the film as body guard to Big
Louis—whom he murders in the film's opening "shot." Thereafter
Tony becomes second in command to Johnny Lovo; and through the
course of the film's action Tony proceeds to expand his own power,
first by establishing Lovo as the chief bootlegger of the South Side,
and then by carrying the battle to the North Side, in clear defiance of
Lovo's explicit orders to the contrary.

Several elements of the film indicate the Oedipal character of this
plot thread and demonstrate its kinship to similar plots in *Tiger Shark*
and *Barbary Coast.* Tony's status as a "son" figure, for example, is
established at least in part by his often noted quality of childishness.
For instance, his two sidekicks—Guino ("little boy") Rinaldo and
Angelo—are both presented as children. When Cesca calls on
Rinaldo in Tony's absence he is cutting out paper dolls, for example.
Indeed, when Cesca first sees Guino, through the "X" formed by the

"Gun play" in Scarface; Tony Camonte (Paul Muni) and "the boys."

balcony outside her bedroom window, he is one of several "children" listening to an organ grinder (among these "children" is a pet monkey: the equation of childishness with mimicry is seen repeatedly in the film). Angelo, likewise, *looks* like a perpetual child, his hat always perched high upon his forehead, and his lack of minimal social skills (he cannot read or write and barely understands how to use a telephone) also marks him as childlike. Tony is only slightly less childish. He shares with Guino and Angelo a kind of minimal vocabulary and a childish mispronunciation of words (pretty = pooty). And his exercise of power is simultaneously playful and brutal, as if he were (as indeed he is) the neighborhood bully. Thus when he first gets his hands on a machine gun he plays with it like a toy, shooting up the pool cues in the First Ward Social Club which serves as Lovo's headquarters. Indeed, as he's on his way out the door to lead an attack on Gaffney's crew, Poppy (Lovo's girl) tosses him a handgun in case his "bean shooter" doesn't work. The connection between gangster brutality and childish game playing is overtly evidenced in the bowling-alley sequence. As Gaffney shows off his bowling skills Tony and "the boys" enter the bowling alley and position themselves among the arcade games, whence Tony then blasts Gaffney. Immediately to Tony's right is a mechanical baseball game, the control of which is shaped remarkably like a pistol grip: "gun play" indeed.

Tony's status as a "son" to Lovo is further reinforced by references to sexuality. Most obviously there is the matter of Tony's relationship with Poppy, Lovo's girl until Tony effectively takes over control of Lovo's gang. Given Tony's childish enthusiasm and Lovo's apparent age and lack of energy, it is easy to see the Tony/Lovo/Poppy triangle in Oedipal terms; as in *Barbary Coast* and *Come and Get It*, father fights son for the attentions of a woman. Indeed, like Louis Chamalis in *Barbary Coast*, Lovo is more concerned to revenge his sexual humiliation at the hands of the son character than he is to maintain his power per se. Thus his control over Tony is always tenuous; but Lovo makes no attempt to counter Tony until Tony openly makes his move for Poppy during the night club sequence.

Equally important, though more difficult to deal with, is the matter of Tony's motives—which are *not* well explained by reference only to his desire for Poppy: Tony's aspirations to power are clearly evident long before his relationship with Poppy heats up. The generally accepted picture of Tony's motives focuses on Tony's status as a kind of Darwinian "primitive." Robin Wood remarks, for instance, that "Tony is introduced as a squat shadow, evoking ape or Neander-thaler" (59). And Kathleen Murphy has suggested that Tony's rise and fall "apes the process of civilization": he begins as a shadow and is next seen in a barber's chair, his face swathed cocoon-like in a hot towel, from whence he is then "born" as a kind of "pre-civilized" example of *homo hawksianus*.[3] Tony's motives are thus read, in general terms, as expressing the savage's will to survive.

A more specific explanation of Tony's motives is possible, however, as evidenced quite clearly by the scar on Tony's face. Poppy asks him about it during the first scene in Lovo's apartment. Tony describes the scar as "old business." And Lovo then interjects that the business took place "with a blonde in a Brooklyn speakeasy." Again we see a connection in Hawks between sexuality and "business" (though the "business" in *Scarface* is of a more malign order than that which is generally seen elsewhere in Hawks). Indeed, there is a good deal of evidence to suggest that the driving force behind Tony's "business" career (Tony describes himself as "a good salesman" before setting out to take "orders"—at gunpoint—for Lovo's bootleg beer) is essentially sexual—even before he sets his sights seriously on Poppy. No sooner does Lovo make a sexually loaded promise that Tony will be his second in command ("stick with me and you'll be walking around in lace pants and a gold hat") than Tony counters by offering Lovo a cigar—which Lovo rejects, handing Tony a cigar of his own. As soon as Tony leaves Lovo's apartment he immediately changes his previously subservient tune: Lovo, he now tells Guino, "is soft." (Lovo later accuses Big Louis of being "soft" in order to justify rubbing him out.) When Lovo complains that Tony is disobeying orders and runs the risk of inviting retaliation from O'Hara's North Side mob, Tony replies that O'Hara "ain't so tough, hanging out in a flower shop—you afraid of a guy like that?" And of course there is the whole issue of Tony's apparently incestuous relationship with his sister Cesca, to which I will return.

The picture we get of Tony's status in the film's initial Oedipal plot is thus clear in its outlines. In certain respects he recalls characters like Spike in *A Girl in Every Port*, Graham in *The Criminal Code*, and Carmichael in *Barbary Coast*: all, Tony included, are boys at heart who evidence an essentially healthy desire to grow up, both socially and sexually. Indeed, Tony is most sympathetic at precisely those moments in the film when his boyish enthusiasm is openly expressive of his own sexuality, when courting Poppy, for example, or even when wondering which of two guys the girl in the play *Rain* will choose. But in other respects Tony also recalls characters such as Brady in *The Criminal Code*, Mike in *Tiger Shark*, and Louis Chamalis in *Barbary Coast*. All, Tony included, are in some way sexually wounded or lacking (Tony is scarred, Brady lacks a wife, Mike lacks a hand); and in all four cases the character's almost psychotic assertion of social power is a cover for sexual anxiety.

The second of the film's two Oedipal plots confirms that Tony's motives are sexually grounded, reflecting not only a desire *for* but a fear *of* sexuality. The key to this second plot is the relationship between Tony and his sister Cesca. The point is made repeatedly in the film that Tony and Cesca are alike; often the point is made by their mother ("All a the time Tony say like that") but finally and most emphatically by Cesca herself in the final scene in Tony's apartment ("You're me and I'm you"). This likeness can be read in two ways. At one level the sense that Cesca is Tony's double points to such films as *A Girl in Every Port, Come and Get It,* and *Land of the Pharoahs*: in every case a central male character is brought to grief by a woman who comes to embody exactly those negative values (of rigidity and greed, for instance) which the man himself has stood or comes to stand for. The man is thus the culpable party, the cause, while the woman is basically an effect. In *Come and Get It*, for instance, Barney Glasgow heeds the capitalist call to "come and get it" at the expense of his relationship with Lotta I; then, twenty-three years later, Lotta's look-alike daughter allows herself to be courted by Barney for financial motives which mirror his own (she wants to escape small town existence) only then to desert him (quite properly) at film's end in favor of his son. Barney's lack of sexual integrity is thus repaid in kind.

We see a similar situation in *Scarface*. Tony spends the entire film asserting his own personality, often regardless of the consequences to others; and Tony comes to grief when Cesca, his double, makes a similar move, courting Guino in Tony's absence despite the probable consequences (consequences, one might add, which are clearly anticipated by Cesca in the song she sings to Guino, about a locomotive gone out of control, *before* Tony arrives at their apartment). In this respect Cesca serves to mirror Tony's actions: she is a projection into the world of the negative aspects of Tony's personality—a "projection" which eventually provides the occasion for Tony's downfall (Murphy, 63).

However, one can also see in Cesca the positive elements of the "funny mixture" which is Tony Camonte. The gangster environment she lives in allows little opportunity for the positive expression of human desires, but Cesca's desires *are* at heart positive: she wants to grow up and be sexual ("I'm 18," she tells Guino defiantly). The conflict between Tony and Cesca is thus paradoxical in the extreme. In the film's primary plot it is Tony, as the son, who personifies positive sexual energies; while it is Lovo, as the father, who stands for "the law," for the repression of Tony's implicitly sexual drives. In the film's secondary Oedipal triangle, however, the roles shift. Now it is Cesca, in her marriage to Guino, who represents the vitality of youthful sexuality, while it is Tony who enacts the role of the father, by denying Cesca's right to be sexual and by killing her lover, his own "little boy," when Cesca dares to defy him. The fatal ambiguity in Tony's motives is therefore evidenced by the fact that he is the only character to figure in both of the film's Oedipal triangles. Tony is at the film's metaphorical center: he is the point where the two plots intersect—hence the cross-shaped scar on his face. To describe Tony's problem in *Scarface* as a matter of regression to a state of natural savagery is therefore misleading. Tony's problem involves, rather, a *denial* of natural processes. As a child Tony wants time to accelerate,

Cesca (Ann Dvorak) confronts Guino (George Raft).

hence his eagerness to grow up; as a parent figure, however, Tony wants time to stop, hence his attempt to deny Cesca's sexual integrity. And it is that denial—rather than an inherently hostile universe— which is most directly responsible for Tony's downfall.

The "X" figure which permeates the visual world of *Scarface* may thus be read as a constant reminder of the basic shape of the film's action and also of the paradox of values personified by Tony Camonte. One can also read the repeated appearances of the "X" figure, however, as a mark of authorial "presence." For Robin Wood, "*Scarface* remains firmly within the conventions of naturalism" (58)—by which I take him to mean that style remains subservient in the film to action. For John Belton, however, "the camera [in *Scarface*] is surprisingly detached from the action" and in this *Scarface* "doesn't much *look* like Hawks' other work."[4] Both of these views of the relationship of style and theme in *Scarface* are, it seems to me, mistaken, and mistaken for essentially the same reason: both assume that the Hawksian norm is one of visual simplicity and authorial self-effacement. A more accurate view of the Hawksian style would focus on the constant though often subtle interplay in Hawks between action and iconography: even in films where camera work and cutting are fairly straightforward, self-consciousness is often evidenced by genre or auteur references—the Von Sternbergian elements in *Barbary Coast* and *Only Angels Have Wings,* for instance, or the references to Huston in *The Big Sleep* or to Capra in *Ball of Fire* and *I Was a Male War Bride* or to Ford in *Sergeant York* and *Red River,* etc. *Scarface* is no exception in this regard. Indeed, critics frequently point to the thematic and stylistic debts which *Scarface* owes to Von Sternberg's *Underworld* (though usually for the purpose of making the Hecht connection).

In one respect it is appropriate, then, to read the visual world of *Scarface* in expressionistic terms, as a nightmare world of darkness and enclosure from which nature is almost totally absent. As a metaphor the cityscape of *Scarface* is thus more appropriately understood, not in relationship to the universe as a whole, but rather in relationship to the minds and motives of the characters who inhabit it. It is *their* world: its limits are their limits. Tony's steel shutters are thus emblematic of the limited state of his consciousness. (The prison setting in *The Criminal Code,* San Francisco in *Barbary Coast,* and the Glasgow mansion in *Come and Get It* can also be understood in psychological terms, as can the pyramid in *Land of the Pharaohs.*) In another respect, however, the style of *Scarface,* especially the several obtrusive instances of moving camera but also the repeated use of the "X" motif and the very direct references (via the "Cook's Tours" sign) to *Underworld,* evidences a consciousness of a world *beyond* the world of *Scarface,* a consciousness which is focused *on* that nightmare world but which remains independent of it. It is precisely for lacking a strong enough sense of and respect for the world outside the limits of his own desires that Tony Camonte comes to ruin. It is typical of the Hawksian style, however, precisely to insist upon such a knowledge, not only in the comedies, where that insistence is expressed playfully, but also in the adventure films, where consciousness of the world outside is likely, as in *Scarface,* to be thematically central.

The Road to Glory (1936)

I have thus far argued that the tendency to read brutality in the Hawksian film-world as an expression of the basic hostility of existence forces us to deny or to ignore the degree to which the Hawksian universe repeatedly sides with those characters who are capable of trusting to it. Certain environments in Hawks, however, often associated with oppressively legalistic or hierarchical social circumstances, make it very difficult for characters to continue to trust in the world and in each other. We see this clearly enough in the world of *Scarface*, where the basic rule of existence is kill or be killed. Another such circumstance seen repeatedly in Hawks is organized warfare. Not surprisingly, then, it is the "war films" of Howard Hawks which provide the strongest evidence for the Hawks-as-tragedian notion. *The Road to Glory* is a good case in point.

In synopsis, indeed, *The Road to Glory* could well be read as a textbook example of a classic Hawks adventure film of the sort described by Peter Wollen. Death is a central fact throughout the film: its "action" consists of movements back and forth between front line World War I trenches and the tenuous security of rear echelon billets. Against the "barren view of life" implied by such circumstances the film does indeed invoke a sense of group solidarity. When the French Army's "Fifth Company, Second Batallion of the Thirty-Ninth Regiment of the Line" moves forward it is often to the tune of a group sing-along; and the sergeants in the outfit are quick to defend their commander, Captain Paul Laroche (Warner Baxter), when his high casualty rates are questioned by uninitiated outsiders like Lieutenant Michel Denet (Fredric March). At film's center, furthermore, there is a sexual triangle, involving Laroche, Denet, and a young nurse (Monique: June Lang), which might be seen to threaten (though indirectly) the group's *esprit de corps*. And the question to be asked and answered in relationship to all this is whether or not (or to what degree) it is warranted to read the hostility in the film as a basic or unalterable condition of human existence generally. Put another way—and to paraphrase Monique's closing lines—why do the characters in *The Road to Glory* have to die?

We can begin to answer the "why" question by considering the thematic relationship between the film's narrative background, i.e., its overall sequential structure, and its two primary subplots. In large-scale terms *The Road to Glory* is structured, like *The Dawn Patrol*, as a series of repeated actions or recurrent *sequences* of actions. Especially striking in this regard are those events associated with the movement of "Laroche's hard bargains" to and from the front line trenches.

The film begins with the arrival of a courier bearing orders. The courier finds Laroche lying exhausted on his cot while Monique, seated nearby, watches over him. After an air raid, replacements arrive (including Denet). Laroche then inspects the troops (among whom he recognizes a previously wounded soldier and also sees an older recruit whom Laroche then excuses from combat duty), after which he delivers a terse speech recounting the history of the unit and its record of valor. Upon finishing his remarks Laroche turns his back to the troops and tosses a handful of aspirin tablets ("rations") into his mouth. When the unit returns from the front, Monique resumes her watch over Laroche. Again orders are given to move up. Again Laroche delivers his speech—and while giving it he once more notices a recruit too old for combat (his own father, it turns out). During the action which follows Laroche is blinded, and with his father undertakes a suicide mission as an artillery spotter. Cut, then, to the rear, where Monique again keeps watch—but now with Denet. He gives her a package from Laroche (as Laroche had given her a rosary in the first such sequence) and then Denet walks out to the steps overlooking the courtyard and delivers the same speech heard earlier—at the conclusion of which Denet turns his back and tosses down a handful of aspirin.

It is tempting to read the narrative structure of *The Road to Glory* in primarily existential terms as dramatizing "a cyclical view of history whose repetitions generate a sense of timelessness."[5] Such a description would certainly accord with a Wollenesque view of the film. "Another cycle has begun"—the killing continues—and the Hawksian group must continue the struggle to survive.[6] I will eventually want to argue that the thematic implications of *Road to Glory* are far more hopeful than such a view of its structure would seem to suggest. But I would not want to deny that the correlation in the film's structure of repetition and death is important to our understanding of the movie.

What must be understood, however, is that repetition in *Road to Glory* is not an exclusively negative circumstance. It is a source of much of the film's considerable humor, for example. The film takes place in 1916—but Sergeant Bouffiou continues to get orders requesting that he acknowledge the receipt of eight camels issued to him in Algeria in 1892. The potentially positive aspect of repetition in *Road to Glory* is best seen, however, in the film's two primary subplots, both of which may be understood as parables of repetitiveness transformed or rigidity transcended.

The first such subplot in *Road to Glory* involves the Laroche/Denet/Monique triangle which recalls in several respects the Oedipal triangles seen elsewhere in Hawks. Laroche, for instance, is clearly cast in the "father" role—by virtue of his military status as company commander (in this he recalls Brady in *Criminal Code* and Chamalis in *Barbary Coast*: all three characters are accustomed to giving orders), by virtue of his tutor/tyro relationship with Lieutenant Denet (a student in civilian life) and also by virtue of his age, which is emphasized both by his haggard looks (especially when compared to Denet's) and by the entrance midway through the film of his own quite elderly father. Monique, likewise, recalls earlier "daughter" figures in Hawks, especially Cesca in *Scarface,* Mary in *Criminal Code*, and Quita in *Tiger Shark*. All four women come from broken or displaced families (all but Monique lack at least one parent, and Monique's family is dependent upon Laroche for support), and in every case the questionable nature of the "father/daughter" relationship is marked by an implication of incest. Hence the emphasis in *Road to Glory* on the rosary which Laroche gives to Monique: it was given to him by someone he "loved very much"—his sister. The comparison with *Tiger Shark*, it is worth remarking, is especially telling in this regard: Monique's relationship with Laroche, like Quita's with Mike, is based almost exclusively on gratitude rather than sexual attraction, a fact which neither woman attempts to hide. In both cases, however, the "father" figure either refuses to acknowledge or is incapable of gracefully accepting the sexual facts of the matter—and when the younger man (Denet in *Road to Glory*) quite properly earns the daughter's affections, the older man becomes embittered, in Mike's case, at least, to the point of madness and attempted murder.

The Oedipal triangle in *The Road to Glory* is thus quite properly compared to those in other early Hawks films: again there is a basic conflict between social authority (Laroche) and sexual integrity (Monique and Denet). But there are crucial differences to be remarked upon as well. Chief among those differences is the degree to which the actions of the father figure in *Road to Glory* are socially rather than psychologically determined. In the earlier films, as we have seen, the father's identification with "the law" is usually correlated in cause/effect terms with some form of sexual anxiety: the father fears sexual inadequacy and he enforces the law so as to deny the sexuality of others. Indeed, in most of these cases the father actively seeks to acquire or to assert that authority—by brute force (Tony in *Scarface*, Chamalis in *Barbary Coast*), by political means (Brady in *The Criminal Code*), by economic means (Barney Glasgow in *Come and Get It*), etc. In *The Road to Glory,* on the other hand, social power is conferred rather than sought out. There is absolutely no sense in which Laroche can be described as desiring or enjoying the duties of command. If anything, Laroche is presented as someone on the verge of breaking down: hence his rations of cognac and aspirin and his troubled sleep. Even his speech to the troops is framed in negative terms: he expects no one to add to the unit's glory but requires that no one detract from its reputation.

The relationship of Laroche with Monique, accordingly, is less a matter of cause than effect. In the wartime context she represents a last link with normal human existence. Without her presence life for Laroche would be nothing *but* a debilitating cycle of orders received and orders given. What Laroche fails to see (until blindness "opens" his eyes) is the degree to which his relationship with Monique is destructive of those values—of human concern and emotional integrity—which Laroche fights to maintain in himself and his men. By depending on Monique, Laroche passes on the burden and the agony: she is as much his victim as he is the victim of those who command him. She is, in her own words, "a veteran." The sexual subplot in *The Road to Glory* can thus be understood as extending the larger social issue—of the potential deadliness of repetition or rigidity—into the realm of personal relationships. Laroche is threatened by circumstances and he in turn threatens Monique—and Denet as well (after learning of the relationship between them). Even here, however, Laroche is far less at fault or blameworthy than characters like Tony Camonte or Mike Mascarenhas. The threat he represents to Monique is clearly unintended and the threat he represents to Denet is almost equally circumstantial. Orders come down to establish an advanced observation post and Laroche quite properly asks for volunteers, implying only by a glance that Denet should undertake to lead the mission.

The second subplot of *The Road to Glory,* involving the relationship between Laroche and *his* father, works in part to restate the themes of repetition and social rigidity seen elsewhere in the film. More specifically, Private "Morain" (Lionel Barrymore) arrives at company headquarters with a rigid notion of the road to military glory ("You call this war? Where's your cavalry charges and your flags to lead 'em on?") and an implicit desire to relive his past. As a fifteen-year-old bugler he "blew the last charge at Sedan"—and he carries his bugle still, in the clear hope of repeating his glorious moment. Laroche's response to his father's presence betrays another sort of rigidity. In seeking to have his father excused from combat duty Laroche repeats an earlier action of his own (Morain and Bouffiou subsequently conspire with the "wind" to blow the orders into the fireplace); but, more importantly, Laroche's motive for doing so clearly involves a rigid sort of personal pride. As Laroche puts it to Denet: "I couldn't let him stay . . . if he had failed." And it is not at all clear whether the honor at stake is that of Private "Morain" or of Laroche himself. Indeed, Laroche and Morain, father and son, may be seen to "repeat" each other. At one point they even trade "orders": Morain orders Laroche not to send him back ("As your father . . .") and in turn Laroche orders "Private Morain" to come to attention.

Taken together the two "personal" plots of *Road to Glory* may be seen in part to reflect the negative view of repetition implied by the film's sequential structure. Indeed, both plots are concerned with various rigidities of thought and behavior; both involve specific threats to human life (Laroche "suggests" that Denet volunteer for the patrol into enemy territory; Morain mistakenly grenades his own troops); and in both cases rigidity is associated with some variety of unnatural familial relationship (the "incestuous" relationship of Laroche to Monique, the subservience of father to son in the Laroche/Morain relationship). It is also true, however, that certain repetitions in *The Road to Glory* function positively by providing characters with "second chances" which enable them to overcome rigidities of thought and action and to recover their faith in themselves and each other. There is little sense in the film that the larger social circumstances will change. The film's mise-en-scène, indeed, implies just the contrary. Most of the film takes place, like *Scarface*, in man-made enclosures of one sort or another (offices, dug-outs, trenches, etc.) and even the natural landscape, what little we see of it, is scarred by bomb craters, barbed wire, and trees stripped bare of leaves. But the film also allows the possibility that characters can in some sense transcend their circumstances, can refuse to give in to the threats of enclosure and rigidity—and it is exactly that sort of self-awareness that the film may be said to celebrate.

The rigidities overcome in *Road to Glory* are specified primarily as those of the film's two father figures—Laroche and Morain. Both men experience a similar loss of faith or courage. In Laroche's case what is lost is his faith in Monique and his respect for Denet. Upon finding the rosary—which he had given to Monique earlier—in Denet's room, Laroche retreats even further into his rock-hard (*la roche* = the rock) persona. He refuses to shake hands with Denet before going into battle and is short tempered with Sergeant Regnier when he discovers that Private Morain did not go to the rear. Laroche clearly feels himself betrayed—and that feeling is largely a function of ignorance. Monique had never promised sexual fidelity to begin with; and Laroche is clearly unaware that Denet had broken off with Monique, out of respect for Laroche and concern for the unit, *before* Laroche found the rosary. A similar ignorance is at work in Morain's case. He persists in a childish faith in the glory of warfare ("There's no such thing as fear—it's only in the mind"); but that faith crumbles when he volunteers for the patrol led by Denet and gets a first hand look at death and dying. Indeed, it's for fear that he tosses the grenade that kills Bouffiou and wounds Denet.

It is not the case for either man, however, that the loss of faith is permanent. To the contrary, both Laroche and Morain get the second chance each needs to overcome ignorance or fear and to thus restore faith in himself and in others. The second chance in Laroche's case is especially fortuitous. He is blinded at the front and seeks medical aid at the same hospital where Denet had gone for the arm wound he received on patrol. Indeed, Laroche arrives just as Denet and Monique embrace; Monique, assuming Laroche has seen them, confesses her love for Denet; and Denet, in turn, explains that he and Monique had "tried to keep away from each other so as not to hurt" Laroche. Laroche thus "catches" Denet and Monique for a second time; but on this occasion the consequence is the restoration of faith rather than the loss of it. The genuine seriousness of the Denet/Monique relationship is evidenced by their open admission of love for each other (it was not a casual affair); and their mutual respect and concern for Laroche is evidenced by the fact that they had tried to break off their relationship for his sake. Laroche then effectively returns the compliment by making his own "break" with Monique. An order is delivered to reestablish the forward observation post—and the order provides Laroche an opportunity to demonstrate a capacity for self-sacrifice akin to that evidenced previously by Denet.

The order also provides "Morain" with a second chance, both as soldier and father. Laroche needs "eyes" so once again Morain volunteers to go into no-man's-land—not, this time, out of a misguided sense of courage; rather, Morain's motives are those of a responsible parent ("I'll be your eyes, son"). To be sure, it is a suicide mission they undertake, but it hardly represents a cynical or meaningless loss of life—at least not in personal terms. One could argue, indeed, that the double suicide of father and son serves to reassert a belief in the natural cycles of life and time—in which sons follow fathers into sexuality (as Denet follows Laroche) and death (as Laroche follows

Morain). By contrast, the social cycle of actions and relationships which determines the film's narrative structure is unnatural precisely for *denying* biological time: soldiers die "before their time" and sexual relationships are either torturous (the Denet/Monique relationship) or simply nonexistent.

Are we warranted, then, to read death and dying in *The Road to Glory* as emblematic of the basic hostility of the Hawksian universe? I think not—unless we are prepared to see death in a priori terms as a denial of life's meaning and significance. All of the "father and the law" films we have been discussing set biological law, represented by generational conflicts of one sort or another, against social law; and grief usually results when social "codes" are allowed to determine human action, especially sexual action—as we see quite clearly in *The Road to Glory*. It is only when characters get in tune with nature by accepting their place in the generative cycle of biological time that harmony is restored. Indeed, even in as "fatalistic" a film as *The Road to Glory* there is a correlation of musical and natural harmony. Denet and Monique meet by chance during an air raid. And while he tries to establish a romantic mood with the help of a piano, rain starts to fall outside, a benevolent rain which stops the air raid and recalls similarly benevolent rain storms seen elsewhere in Hawks (*Paid to Love, Barbary Coast, Ball of Fire, I Was a Male War Bride,* etc.). To accept biological fact, of course, is still to accept the fact of death. But death in Hawks is very seldom the result of natural causes. It is far more often a matter of people killing people—often for the very purpose of denying biological time. That, too, could be occasion for a cynical world view. But the fact that chaos is socially motivated in Hawks is ultimately a positive circumstance in the world of films. *If* people are doing it wrong—*then* people can get it right.Indeed, it is exactly that sort of rightness which is celebrated in Denet's decision to repeat Laroche's speech to the troops. There is little if any sense of despair involved, of having given in to an inevitable fate. Rather, Denet's recitation and his gesture of taking the handful of aspirin is to be read largely as a tribute to Laroche, as a recognition of the positive human qualities which Laroche has stood for both in life and death. There is nothing cynical about it.

Red River (1948)

The issue of "society" in Hawks is generally discussed in relation to the concept of the "Hawksian group." The point is frequently made, for example, that groups in Hawks are often made up of exiles or expatriates who seem bent on rejecting civilization (and women) in

Addressing the troops in The Road to Glory: *(top) Warner Baxter as Capt. Laroche; (bottom) Fredric March as Lt. Denet.*

favor of a more primitive and masculine countersociety. In the case of *Red River*, however, focusing exclusively on relationships within the group clearly requires one to ignore much that makes the film thematically and cinematically interesting.

Robin Wood, for one, is quite open in deciding to ignore or downplay the epic quality of *Red River*. In the *Focus!* version of his *Red River* essay Wood attributes the historical elements of the film to genre conventions ("*Red River* is in the mainstream western tradition") and in the book version of the same essay he refines the point by attributing the "growth-of-civilization theme" largely to the influence of Bordon Chase—who wrote the original story and cowrote the screenplay.[7] It follows, then, in light of the Chase/Hawks dispute over the ending of the film, that we are justified in attending primarily to the film's "more personal, psychological issues" (Wood, 124). Accordingly, Wood's discussion plays down the film's narrative framework (involving the first cattle drive from Texas to Kansas on the Chisholm Trail) and focuses instead on the issue of character motivation: more specifically, why doesn't Tom Dunson (John Wayne) fulfill his vow to kill his "adopted son" (Matthew Garth: Montgomery Clift) in revenge for Garth's seizure of Dunson's "Red River D" herd?

For critics like Robert Sklar and Raymond Durgnat, on the other hand, *Red River* "is rich in social significance."[8] It is a film about the issues of empire in which the "human themes" are "subordinate to even more fundamental issues of economic survival" (Sklar, 169). According to Sklar, "*Red River* is a film about cows, horses, gun play, brave women, daring men—and capitalism" (169). Indeed, it is "Hawks's boldest celebration of the capitalist system" (Durgnat, 13).

There are problems, it seems to me, with each of these two lines of argument on *Red River*. The justification for explicitly ignoring *any* element of a film, for example, is on principle a weak one. There *are* cases where we have little choice in the matter. The scene midway through *Scarface* where a sedately impassioned group of citizens confronts a newspaper editor over the amount of publicity given to gangsters is clearly out of tune with the rest of the film. Thematically, stylistically, it doesn't belong. Indeed, it was inserted to forestall criticism of the film after Hawks left the project (see Belton, 20). But there is nothing even remotely like this in *Red River*. The epic quality of the film—both visually and thematically—is a constant and integral part of *Red River*, regardless of any sense we might have that it is atypical of Hawks. The film's epic elements cannot be ignored.

But of course *Red River* is typical—and in at least two important respects. Thematically, *Red River* can be seen as yet another variant of the Oedipal fable in Hawks, and it is characteristic of these films, as we have seen, to raise explicitly social issues in the context of largely personal relationships: the father *is* the law—or at least would like to think so. Thus there is no *necessary* antithesis between personal and social concerns in Hawks, however much the standard view of his films encourages us to think so. Indeed, conflict arises in Hawks precisely when personal and social imperatives are at odds.

The stylistic dimension of *Red River*, furthermore, is also typically Hawksian and also serves to raise the issue of social relationships. Like many if not most Hawks films, that is, *Red River* relies heavily upon genre iconography. Hence some of the confusion. The reference points are seldom constant from one film to the next. We are reminded of Lubitsch here, of Keaton there, of Wellman, Capra, Von Sternberg, Ford, Eisenstein (in *Viva Villa!*), etc. But the repeated use of genre and director references serves not only to multiply connotations but also to raise the issue of "film language." We are constantly reminded in Hawks of the larger symbolic system of which each individual film is a particular part—and implicit in that system is a self-conscious "speaker" (self-conscious in the sense that he seems clearly aware of a world beyond the world of his own work) and an "audience." Indeed, to the degree that *Red River* invites us to respond to its connotations we become active members of a community of significance. Our relationship to the film is itself an implicitly "social relationship"—a point clearly emphasized in *Red River* by the fact of Walter Brennan's voice-over first-person narration.[9]

To argue that *Red River* is centrally concerned with social relationships is not necessarily to agree with those critics who see the film as an "apologia for capitalism." Such an approach runs the risk of degenerating into caricature: hence, for example, Durgnat's description of Dunson as a "Captain Bligh–cattle baron" and of Matthew Garth as a "pacifist-reformist." Such an either/or approach clearly *over-generalizes*: it fails to account for the fact that *Red River* presents us with a range of social models, various *kinds* of capitalisms.

Thus at one extreme is the venture capitalism of Tom Dunson, which the film clearly portrays as antisocial. At film's beginning Dunson (with Groot: Walter Brennan) pulls out of the wagon train in order to head off on his own. In so doing he clearly disregards both the safety of others (Indian attacks are expected; the wagonmaster tells Dunson he's "too good a gun to let leave the train") and the sexual and emotional integrity of Fen, the girl he leaves behind, as well—despite the courage and fortitude she demonstrates in pleading her love and her cause. Indeed, the long shot of Fen as she stands alone on the prairie, with the wagons rolling along behind her, conveys a sense of dignity which contrasts sharply with Dunson's legalistic justification for leaving the train ("I signed nothing. If I had, I'd stay").

Another extreme (both logical and geographical) in the range of social models in *Red River* is provided by the mercantile capitalism which characterizes the end of the Chisholm Trail—the railhead at Abilene, Kansas. The immediate reason for undertaking the cattle drive is a lack of southern markets. The Civil War, as Groot tells Matthew, "took all the money out of the South." The arrival of Dunson's herd at Abilene thus represents a restoration of economic and social bonds—and a restoration, also, of economic and social options: Matt is free to bargain with a number of cattle traders (this freedom contrasts strongly with Dunson's practice: he rounds up "everything that walks" before starting the drive, regardless of brand, effectively forcing other ranchers to bargain on his terms). Furthermore, it is also worth remarking that Abilene is not presented as just *any* railhead. The entrance of the herd into town, to the accompaniment of a dancing fiddler, is presented as a joyous if somewhat raucous event, the whole recalling the Independence Day parade and festivities in Ford's *Young Mr. Lincoln*; and the cattle trader who comes out to meet the herd is played by Harry Carey—whose roles in early Ford Westerns, in previous Hawks films (*Barbary Coast, Air Force*), and in Capra (he played the Vice President in *Mr. Smith Goes to Washington*) identify him as an icon of democratic honesty, integrity, and fair dealing.

A third social model in *Red River* is provided by various manifestations of the Hawksian group. One such group is the wagon train that Dunson deserts in the film's opening scene. The scene's focus, of course, is on Dunson and his motives for leaving; but his departure, and the subsequent attack on the train by Indians, raises one of the film's central issues: the relationship between social unity and human survival. Another such group—raising the same issues—is the wagon train of gamblers and saloon girls (including Tess Millay) which Matt and his drovers come to the defense of *after* wresting control of the herd from Dunson: again we see an equation between communal (and sexual) action and human survival. (It is worth remarking that the equation works both ways: the Indians who attack the train can also be seen as a community striving for survival.)

Clearly the most important of these Hawksian groups, however, is the crew of cattle hands who sign on to help Dunson make the drive to market. Indeed, they are something *more* than mere cow hands.

When Dunson formally proposes the drive and asks the men to sign up he addresses them in ambiguous terms, as employees ("Nobody has to come along. I'll still have a job for you when we get back.") but also as victims, like Dunson himself, of the social conditions brought on by the war ("You came back to nothing. You found your homes gone, your cattle scattered, your land stolen by carpetbaggers"). In potential, at least, each of the drovers is thus Dunson's equal, someone who once was a rancher and who hopes to be again. As Teeler puts it to Dunson, after attempting to leave the drive: "This herd don't belong to you. It belongs to every poor hopin' and prayin' cattleman in the whole wide state." Even in revolt, to be sure, the cattle drovers exist within capitalist extremes; but it is also true that Dunson's sort of venture-capital fervor (as is often the case in Hawks) is called into genuine question for so seriously contradicting the implicitly democratic and communal spirit in which the drive began. The group's problem has little to do, therefore, with "preserving its exclusivity" apart from the larger society. Rather, it is the preservation of community *within* the group, and the preservation of the group *within* society, which is at stake in *Red River*.

The chief problem with reading *Red River* as an apology for capitalism is not, however, the tendency to overgeneralize by failing to distinguish the various social models employed in the film. The real flaw in such a reading lies in the opposite direction: in refusing to generalize *enough*. To call *Red River* a capitalist movie is ultimately to trivialize it by limiting the significance of the film to that of its genetic context. *Red River* thus becomes primarily an historical document the existence of which is explained in economic or ideological terms: *Red River* is the signifier, "capitalism" is the signified. One can readily argue, however, that such a reading represents a premature "naturalization" of the text and premature for refusing to consider the degree to which capitalism may itself be read as a signifier—as a metaphor—at which point we confront once again the question of the relationship between the film's economic background and the more personal though no less social action which occupies the foreground of the frame and of our attention.

In discussing *Barbary Coast* I drew a distinction between "society" and "monopoly capitalism" in Hawks—and I went on to suggest that in criticizing the latter Hawks need not be read as rejecting the former (though such readings are common). We see a similar situation in *Red River*. Monopoly capitalism of the Tom Dunson sort is clearly called into question—not only to the obvious extent that it results in several deaths and in the eventual mutiny of the drovers, but also inasmuch as Dunson's brand of capitalism stands in clear contrast to the other social models provided by the film. The issue in *Red River* need not be read, then, as a matter of capitalism per se. What is at issue, rather, are those negative aspects of capitalism—and by extension of social organizations generally—which are personified by the character of Tom Dunson. Why must Dunson be over-thrown? And why is he eventually forgiven—and forgiving?

We can begin to answer the first of these two questions by refer-ence to the issue of movement. The thematic importance of move-ment is implicit in the film's journey structure; and when the mutiny comes it comes primarily over the issue of direction. While many factors are involved, the key incident which precipitates the revolt against Dunson is the entrance into the trail camp of a strange drover, a survivor of another trail drive that had been ambushed by Missouri border gangs. The man can barely talk for the rope burns on his neck, but he says enough to confirm the rumors that the route which Dunson is set on following is hazardous. Moreover, he also confirms the report by Cherry Valance that the railhead has moved west to Abilene, providing an alternate goal and therefore an alternative route. But Dunson refuses (once again) to change direction.

The direction issue—and Dunson's apparent inability to change his mind or his route—is raised, however, even as early as the film's first scene, when Dunson pulls out of the wagon train. But it is not simply a matter of Dunson deserting the train. Rather, mise-en-scène estab-lishes directionality, both within the frame and through it, as one of the film's primary metaphors. Thus when Dunson and Fen embrace, Dunson is facing screen right and Fen screen left: she begs him to change his mind "just once" but he refuses. And when he sub-sequently pulls his wagon away from the rest of the train, the scene is photographed in long shot, thus emphasizing directionality: the wagon train rolls right to left behind Fen while Dunson's wagon moves left to right out of the frame. The metaphor may be read as follows: movement right to left, both in the opening scene and throughout the film, is correlated by and large with group action, with teamwork (the drive is framed by two extended right-to-left pan shots; the river crossing moves from right to left; the drovers ride into the embattled wagon train from right to left, etc.); movement left to right, however, both in the opening scene and in subsequent scenes, is typically correlated with idiosyncrasy, with preestablished plans, and eventually with death (Dunson typically occupies the left side of

the frame; in each of the gunfights Dunson shoots from left to right;
etc.). The hazardous aspect of such idiosyncrasy is perhaps best
evidenced in the stampede sequence: the stampede starts because
Bunk Kenelly (like Dunson) is incapable of controlling his appetite
(he reaches for the sugar once too often and upsets the chuck-wagon
tinware), and once started the herd moves left to right in a relentless
surge of destructiveness.

Another kind of idiosyncrasy is evidenced by Dunson's self-serving
use of language. Robert Sklar, for example, makes much of Dunson's
devotion to contracts: not signing on enables Dunson to desert the
group in the film's first scene, and the signed contract for the cattle
drive is Dunson's justification for killing later on (173). "There'll be no
quitting," Dunson had said in proposing the venture, and he doesn't
hesitate to enforce that prediction by gunplay. It's here that Dunson
recalls other father figures in Hawks. "I'm the law," he says before
preparing to hang Teeler—and his identification with "the law" is
reinforced by his habit of "reading" scripture over his victims. As the
Hank Worden character puts it: "Why when you've killed a man, why
try to read the Lord in as a partner in the job?" The point to make,
however, is that Dunson (like Chamalis in *Barbary Coast*) only
honors language so far. He does not hesitate to take Don Diego's land
by force, despite Diego's clear and legal title to it; and, more importantly, Dunson refuses to believe reports that the railhead has moved
to Kansas ("I've seen buyers and cash in Sedalia—what have you seen
in Abilene?"). Perhaps Dunson's "hardness" is best symbolized by
the image of the branding iron with which he lays a kind of "linguistic"
claim to his empire.

It is not capitalism by itself, then, which is at issue in *Red River*—
unless we are inclined to believe that capitalism always displays a
Dunson-like face. In the world of *Red River*, however, Dunson's
desire to establish his ranch and the courage he demonstrates in
deciding to drive his cattle to market are clearly to be respected. Matt
insists, for example, that the check for the herd be made out to
Dunson. What *is* at issue is Dunson's *way* of doing it. From the very
beginning Dunson's positive motives are set in a context of negative
consequences almost all of which follow from Dunson's increasingly
rigid inability to acknowledge some aspect of the world outside
himself. Thus in leaving the wagon train Dunson leaves Fen behind:
he cannot admit to needing what "a woman can give." Likewise,
when the time comes to establish a brand Dunson fails to include an
"M" for Matthew Garth, despite the fact that it is Matthew's cow

Directionality and mise-en-scène: from left to right in Red River.

which will make the herd possible. Indeed, it is because Dunson hasn't actually seen the railhead in Abilene that he refuses to change the direction of the drive. None of these denials is *necessary* to the larger task of establishing Dunson's ranch. On the contrary, in refusing to change direction Dunson clearly jeopardizes his chances for success. But all of these denials on Dunson's part *are* typical of the figure of the Hawksian father who sees the world almost totally in terms of his own needs and plans. As we have seen, however, such plans by themselves tend to become psychological traps in Hawks, traps which are only escaped by accepting the world and trusting to it.

There is a sense, however, in which Dunson may be described as never having forgotten the world outside—and it is that inability to forget which accounts for his ruthlessness but also for his eventual reconciliation with Matthew. More specifically, Dunson seems incapable of forgetting Fen. Matthew, for instance, serves as a constant reminder of Fen's death. He was part of the same wagon train as Fen; he wears the bracelet which Dunson had given to Fen and which Dunson subsequently took from the wrist of a dead brave; Dunson clearly sees Matthew as the "son" he and Fen might have had if she had survived (in parting, Dunson had promised to send for her). There is, furthermore, a clear correlation between Dunson's increasing obstinacy and the guilt he feels for Fen's death. Both Matt and Groot repeatedly tell Dunson "you was wrong," thereby echoing Fen's line in the film's first scene ("You're wrong")—and the more they say it the more set Dunson becomes in his ways. Perhaps Dunson's sensitivity to Fen's memory is best evidenced by his conversation late in the film with Tess Millay (Joanne Dru). Dunson is on Matt's trail and comes across her wagon train eight days after Matt and the herd have gone. The entire conversation echoes the film's first scene. But the point to emphasize here involves the degree to which Dunson responds to the echoes, as if he had never forgotten a word of his last conversation with Fen: he even completes the sentence ("You felt like you had knives sticking in you") when Tess tries to describe how she felt when Matt left her to take Dunson's herd on to Abilene. Dunson's identification with the law is thus very much akin in its genesis to similar identifications elsewhere in Hawks: in nearly every case devotion to legal or social power is a reaction to feelings of sexual inadequacy or guilt. The fact of Dunson's guilt, however, also allows us to understand the logic behind the film's resolution, especially to the extent that Dunson's guilt evidences, however indirectly, a capacity on Dunson's part for attending to a world beyond the world of his own immediate desires.

The latter third of *Red River* has been much criticized—for the almost slapstick quality of the reconciliation scene between Dunson and Garth, but also, and more significantly, for the introduction so late into the film of the Tess Millay character. Even Robin Wood, whose defense of the film's ending is hard to better, considers Tess's relationships with Garth and Dunson "contrived" (123). In the present context, however, it is possible to see Tess as a striking but nevertheless typical embodiment of the general benevolence of the Hawksian universe. As Kathleen Murphy points out, the cattle drive from Texas to Kansas both duplicates and reverses, with important variations, the initial journey from Missouri to Texas (224). More specifically, after Matt takes over the drive he is given repeated opportunity to relive Dunson's past and thereby to relieve Dunson, by proxy, of the guilt which had hardened his feelings. Thus Matt is given the choice between protecting the herd and riding to the rescue of Tess's wagon train. Matt does not repeat Dunson's error. Rather than desert the train he chooses (unlike Dunson) to stay and defend it. Indeed, in defending it he fights side by side with Tess Millay, and before leaving Matt repeats another of Dunson's actions by giving Tess the bracelet which Dunson had originally given Fen. Matt and the herd then move on—but even here Matt's actions and motives differ significantly from those which Dunson evidenced in leaving Fen fifteen years earlier. Matt has a real herd to take to market; Dunson only had an idea. And when Matt tells Tess that she is too weak to travel it is not altogether a mark of his own insecurity: Tess sustained an arrow wound in the Indian attack and really does need to rest. Furthermore, Matt knows full well that Dunson must be close behind.

By the time Dunson arrives at the wagon train, then, circumstances have made Tess a genuine reembodiment of Fen; and by talking to her Dunson is enabled to gain a necessary perspective on his own history and actions. To be sure, Dunson does not change his mind on the spot. But he changes it enough to grant Tess's request (echoing Fen's) that he take her with him to Abilene—and that becomes the first step in an almost inevitable process of renewal. Indeed, Dunson is sitting screen right throughout the conversation with Tess (thus, literally, reversing his position) and this change of direction is reinforced in the final showdown when Dunson makes his famous long walk through the herd: from *right to left*.

The positive effect of Tess's intervention is clearly visible, then, even before Dunson and Matt finally square off. Tess's stepping in to stop the fist fight which erupts when Matt refuses to draw his gun thus

Reversing position in Red River: *John Wayne as Tom Dunson with (top) Fen (Coleen Gray) and (bottom) Tess Millay (Joanne Dru).*

represents simply one more step in the process by which Dunson is reintegrated into the group and into society. Indeed, by the end of the fight Dunson and Matt are encircled by the trail drive crew. Once again Dunson is prevented from enforcing "the law": but Dunson no longer *needs* to enforce it. In telling Matt that he'd "better marry that girl" Dunson effectively acknowledges and is thereby relieved of the guilt he felt for deserting Fen: he cannot bring her back but he can discourage Matt from repeating his own mistake. The point to emphasize, however, is not simply the fact that Tess intervenes, but rather the fact that Dunson *accepts* her intervention. By so doing Dunson exhibits a willingness to trust in the world and in other people; and it's that sort of willingness, in *Red River* no less than elsewhere, which is the chief prerequisite to Hawksian societies, whether capitalist or not.

5

Women in Hawks

CRITICAL DISCUSSIONS OF WOMEN in the films of Howard Hawks tend to focus on two kinds of evidence: formal evidence and presentational evidence. To discuss the "Hawksian woman" in formal terms is to consider her function *within* the specific thematic matrix of any given film. Thus the standard view of Hawks makes a generic distinction between Hawks's adventure films and his comedies. Women, accordingly, are discussed *in relation to* the larger thematic connotations which are commonly attributed to the genres: women in the adventure films function formally as *threats* to group unity, while in the comedies women are seen as *threats* to masculinity itself.

My own practice in the present discussion has also been to see each film in formal or thematic terms, though my view of the films, and, therefore, of the parts played in them by women, differs in certain important respects from that proposed by Peter Wollen and others. Briefly, I have argued that women in Hawks function less as threats than as *victims*. Men in Hawks tend often to fear sexuality and maturity and they express that fear by trivializing or denying the sexual and human integrity of female characters. In some films (*A Girl in Every Port* and *Scarface,* for instance) men suffer for their actions—often at the hands of women who have themselves been forced to experience rejection. More commonly, however, the women function as embodiments of a benevolent universe— especially to the extent that they offer to male characters the "second chances" they need to redeem their previous sexual misdeeds. Thus in *The Criminal Code* it is the love affair between Brady's daughter and the convict which gives Brady the chance he needs to disavow the legal code which wrongly condemned Graham to prison in the first

The Hawksian Woman: (top) Katharine Hepburn with Cary Grant in Bringing Up Baby *(1938) and (bottom) Barbara Stanwyck with Gary Cooper in* Ball of Fire *(1941).*

place. Thus it is Bonnie Lee in *Only Angels Have Wings* who gives Jeff the opportunity to break out of his iron-man flyer persona. Thus it is Tess Millay in *Red River* who gives Dunson the second chance he needs to redeem his earlier cruelty to Fen. It is the task of the present chapter to extend this view of sexual relationships in Hawks by considering some of the social and psychological terms in which women are generally presented in his films. What are the distinctive presentational attributes of the "Hawksian woman" and how do those attributes contribute to the thematic or formal logic of the films in question?

Dependence, Independence, and Professionalism

It is commonly assumed that the emotional and ethical independence so frequently demonstrated by women in Hawks is primarily a function of economic status. Many of them, like Bonnie Lee in *Only Angels Have Wings* or Feathers in *Rio Bravo,* are professionals of one sort or another who are capable of maintaining themselves without depending directly on men. "In this," writes Naomi Wise, "lies their special maturity and integrity. Since they are independent, self-supporting, and competent, their choices are made by personal will rather than by social or economic pressure."[1]

I would hardly wish to discount the relevance of class matters relative to women in Hawks. Ultimately, however, I do not believe that class alone determines the emotional and ethical worth of the Hawksian woman. Put another way, women in Hawks clearly exist in a variety of class contexts. Many are almost completely dependent upon men; others are financially well off. Few Hawksian women, however, are genuine professionals; and it is seldom their professional skill which is at issue in any case. On the contrary, the issue in the vast majority of Hawks films is precisely a matter of human as opposed to professional worth. It is when the worth and integrity of women are denied that trouble generally follows in Hawks, as we have seen in *Only Angels Have Wings, Red River,* and *I Was a Male War Bride.*

A large number of women in Hawks—contrary to the accepted picture—exist in very negative economic circumstances. Several such women we have already considered: Dolores in *Paid to Love,* Tessie in *A Girl in Every Port,* Mary in *Barbary Coast.* Two further examples of this character type must suffice.

Lee Merrick (Ann Dvorak) in *The Crowd Roars* is an important example of "dependency" in Hawks. I remarked earlier upon the narrative logic of *The Crowd Roars*. The James Cagney character, Joe Greer, is an auto racer whose fear of mortality and maturity is evidenced primarily in the relationship he maintains with his younger brother. He discourages Eddie from driving in the first place, and when Eddie proves himself on the track Joe does his dehumanizing best to deny Eddie (and himself) the company of women, especially that of his own fiancée, Lee Merrick, and of her close friend Anne (Joan Blondell). Indeed, Joe calls both women "tramps" at one point and accuses Anne of gold-digging when she falls in love with Eddie.

Joe's eventual rejection of Lee, then, has financial as well as sexual consequences. She and Joe had been living together without being married, and she clearly depends upon Joe for financial support. It's either that or go to work, like Anne, as a shop girl. Lee's strength of character is thus severely tested when Joe cuts her off. Rather than give up on Joe, however, Lee borrows train fare to Indianapolis and takes a job as a greasy-spoon waitress in the hope that Joe, however down and out, will still show up for the Indy 500. Her doing so is thus doubly significant. On the one hand it confirms the fact that her feelings for Joe are *not* dependent upon financial circumstances and never really had been. She maintains her emotional integrity, that is, *regardless* of her financial situation. More importantly, Lee's action also evidences a willingness on her part, however meager her resources, to let Joe depend upon her: again, emotional integrity is divorced from economic circumstances.

A more negative example of financial dependency in Hawks is provided by Lotta Morgan (Frances Farmer) in *Come and Get It*. Lotta, like Dolores in *Paid to Love* and Mary in *Barbary Coast*, is a prototypical Hawksian "saloon girl," self-assuredly, self-consciously sexual (especially when singing à la Dietrich) but clearly unhappy with her circumstances. Her rendition of "Aura Lee," for instance, provides a vision of sexual fulfillment ("Sunshine on my face was he") which serves as an ironic comment on the sexual role she plays while singing it. Indeed, just before beginning the song she bargains with the saloonkeeper to drug Barney Glasgow's beer: Barney had won $500 in a shell game and Lotta offers to help get it back—in exchange, it turns out, for the $200 she needs for railroad fare to go home. When Glasgow offers to bankroll her departure, however, she knocks over

Frances Farmer as Lotta in Come and Get It.

the drugged beer and joins him in the tray-flinging brawl which follows when Barney tries to leave.

It cannot be said, then, that Lotta allows her financial circumstances to determine altogether her sense of self. Even while acting the saloon-girl part she evidences a strong measure of ironic detachment (Barney: "So you're not lucky, eh?" Lotta: "You think I'd be here if I was?"). But it is equally clear that Lotta would prefer to live otherwise. Indeed, after Barney skips out on her (to marry the daughter of his business partner) Lotta agrees to marry Swan Bostrom rather than continue playing the saloon-girl role. (We see a similar pattern of action and motive in *Tiger Shark* when Quita agrees to marry Mike Mascarenhas—partly, like Lotta, for reasons of gratitude, but also to escape the prospect of prostitution.)

One does not hesitate to describe women like Lotta Morgan and Quita Silva as being, in economic terms, "lower class." In such cases class status clearly weighs against personal and sexual integrity, though women in Hawks seldom break under the strain. A large number of women in Hawks must be described, however, as "upper class." Fabienne in *Fazil* is an heiress, for example. Mary Brady in *The Criminal Code* is the daughter of a prison warden. The Joan Crawford character in *Today We Live* is the daughter of an established British family (we first see her in the family mansion). The Fay Wray character in *Viva Villa!* is the sister of a rich Mexican landowner. Susan Vance in *Bringing Up Baby* has a millionaire aunt. Nellifer in *Land of the Pharaohs* is a princess, as is Teal Eye in *The Big Sky*. And Easy Mueller in *Man's Favorite Sport?* is the daughter of the owner of a fishing resort.

Even here, however, there is reason to believe that class status weighs against personal integrity. Wealth, that is, enables such women to act with remarkable style and self-assurance. But self-assurance apparently dictates a break with class when it comes to choosing a sexual partner. In nearly every case such women in Hawks establish sexual relationships which cut across lines of class, culture, or nationality. Fabienne is French but marries an Arab. Mary Brady falls in love with a convict. Diana Boyce-Smith (Joan Crawford) is torn between her childhood sweetheart (Robert Young) and the American flyer played by Gary Cooper in *Today We Live*. Fay Wray is attracted to Wallace Beery's Pancho Villa in *Viva Villa!* In *Bringing Up Baby* Susan Vance falls in love with a scientist who is clearly out of place in her upper-class milieu. Likewise, Teal Eye in *The Big Sky* picks a white man with an almost racist hatred of Indians for her husband, as if attracted by his antagonism.

Perhaps the defining instances here are seen in *The Big Sleep*. General Sternwood has two daughters, "both pretty and both pretty wild." The taste of the younger daughter runs to chauffeurs and racketeers while her older sister, Vivian (Lauren Bacall), becomes involved with private investigator Philip Marlowe (Bogart), a working-class version of her upper-class adventurer father. The contrast between the sisters is crucial. Carmen, the younger, is clearly a headstrong child in a woman's body whose refusal to grow up ("You ought to wean her, she's old enough") is equated with death (did she or didn't she kill Sean Regan?) and madness. Vivian, on the other hand, clearly plays the parent role vis-à-vis Carmen, doing her best to keep Carmen out of trouble. She thus accepts responsibility for her father's self-acknowledged parental misdeeds (she therefore embodies his "second chance") but it is a responsibility she cannot shoulder alone: hence the relationship she eventually develops with

Marlowe. Both, in some sense, are revolutionaries who refuse to give in to the impotent hothouse morality which is regretted (to his credit) by the General but which is exploited by characters such as crime boss Eddie Mars. In the face of class decadence "insubordination" is the only viable stance—both ethically and sexually.

Being "good, awful good," as the Bacall character in *The Big Sleep* makes clear, is not in Hawks a function of professionalism per se. It has to do rather with qualities of self-possession, of intelligence, of courage, of responsibility, etc. Nevertheless, a number of women in Hawks *are* independent professionals, and in nearly every case their professionalism is important not only as a test of their abilities but also for raising the issue of the relationship between sexual facts and social roles.

The sex/role relationship in Hawks is most clearly at issue in those films wherein women play roles traditionally fulfilled by men. Such women are relatively few in number, however, and the fact of their professionalism is not always borne down on. Put another way, the professional competency of women in Hawks is often assumed as a matter of course; it is less a source of independence than a sign of it.

An early example of female professionalism in Hawks is the character of Tommy (June Travis) in *Ceiling Zero*. When we first see her she is at the controls of an airplane and throughout the film she is treated as an integral part of the "Federal Aviation" crew. Nevertheless, it is not her professionalism which is at issue: she is only a student pilot. Thus it is her ambition rather than her skill which leads to her relationship with Dizzy Davis (James Cagney). Her ambition to be a pilot, however, represents a clear break with sex-role expectations of the sort seen elsewhere in the film (all the other women are wives): hence, perhaps, her masculine nickname, and hence as well her sexual aggressive vis-à-vis Dizzy,, offering to spend the night with him after the crash-related death of his close friend Tex Clarke.

A similar correlation of female professionalism and sexual self-confidence is evidenced by the character of Dallas (Elsa Martinelli) in *Hatari!*—though once again emotional worth is *not* defined exclusively in professional terms. *Hatari!* takes place in Africa; the Hawksian group headed by Sean Mercer (John Wayne) is in the business of capturing animals for zoos; Dallas is a professional photographer on assignment from the Swiss zoo that buys most of the group's catch. Sean's initial impulse is to send her packing—not because she is unprofessional on her own terms but because she is an amateur on his ("Have you ever been hunting? Have you ever been to Africa?").

Even here, however, "professionalism" is not really at issue. Dallas is quickly welcomed into the group by everyone *except* Sean; his acceptance is slower in coming because of a previous negative experience with a woman. But in neither case is it professional ability per se which earns Dallas the respect of others.

For everyone other than Sean, indeed, it is her ability to apologize for her inexperienced performance on her first capture run (she cannot stand up in the bouncing capture truck) which insures her inclusion in the group. And Sean's respect and affection are earned in stages; first by her willingness to buck accepted practice when she prevents a game warden from shooting an orphaned baby elephant; then by her willingness to take the sexual initiative with Sean despite his gruff defensiveness ("Sean, how do you like to kiss?"); and finally by her willingness, qualified though it is by exasperation, to undergo initiation into the Warushi tribe as "Mama Tembo"—Sean respects her for the respect she shows the Warushi. To a certain extent, to be sure, Dallas thus becomes a "native," someone like Brandy, the young woman who owns the capture business, who clearly is at home in Africa. But doing so does not require Dallas to give up her own professional identity: she continues to take and develop photographs throughout the film. It is simply that her professionalism represents only one aspect of her person. What matters most in *Hatari!*, not only for Dallas but for everyone, is the ability to get in tune with each other (by way of song, for instance) and with nature—professionalism is only one metaphor among several for that sort of ability.

His Girl Friday (1940)

Hildy Johnson (Rosalind Russell) in *His Girl Friday* is an exceptional example of female professionalism in Hawks—in that her professional dedication and her sense of sexual commitment are far more closely related than is often the case in Hawks's work. Much of the difficulty that critics have had with the film, indeed, can be traced to this somewhat atypical relationship between sex and profession. Two charges, to be specific, are frequently leveled at *His Girl Friday*: (1) that "the political implications of the story are defused by the comedy-romance plot";[2] and (2) that the choice offered Hildy— between the "irresponsibility" personified by her ex-husband, ex-editor Walter Burns (Cary Grant) and the bourgeois respectability personified by her insurance salesman fiancé, Bruce Baldwin (Ralph Bellamy)—"is much too narrow to be acceptable."[3]

The first of these two charges is clearly predicated not only on the general (though questionable) assumption that politics are more important than romance, regardless of context, but also on the additional premise that the film's political plot (involving the escape and recapture of Earl Williams) and its romantic plot (involving, as it were, the "escape and recapture" of Hildy Johnson) bear no thematically significant relationship to one another. The latter assumption is clearly false. The key equation here is that of joblessness with madness or death. At the film's beginning Earl Williams is a political pawn whose execution, for the crime of killing a black cop, has been repeatedly delayed by the mayor (Clarence Kolb) in order to garner the black vote in the upcoming election. But the real issue, as the film presents it, is that of Williams's sanity. Thus a psychiatrist must certify that Williams is sane before he can be executed—and it is during the examination that Williams, thanks to the loan of Sheriff Hartwell's revolver, makes his escape.

It is already clear, however, that Williams is far from sane. He is presented largely as a helpless innocent (consider the visual contrast between his hapless expressions and demeanor and the grotesquely oversized cage where he is kept), and his lack of mental balance is emphasized by his willingness to accept Hildy's suggestion (expressing her intuitive sense of the degree to which Earl has been "ill-used") that Earl had pulled the trigger because guns are examples of "production for use." The cause of Earl's madness is also clear. As one of Hildy's pressroom colleagues puts it, Williams was a bookkeeper who "starts in at $20 a week and after 14 years he gradually works himself up to $17.50." The company he works for "goes out of business and Williams loses his job." After which, it is strongly implied, Earl became unhinged. Earl can thus be read as an instance of the madness which follows when people cease to play social roles which they find meaningful. He therefore personifies the fate which awaits Hildy Johnson (not, it is worth noting, Hildy "Burns") if she gives up the newspaper game. By the same token, however, Hildy can be seen as an exemplar of social sanity in a world gone politically mad—she represents Earl's "second chance" (in that her "production for use" notion can arguably be said to have prompted Earl's escape). That Hildy is there when Earl needs her (as he is there when she needs him) only lends further credence to the thesis that the Hawksian cosmos is essentially benevolent.

The complaint that the choice presented to Hildy is "too narrow to be acceptable" is somewhat less problematic. In terms of mise-en-scène the world of *His Girl Friday* is far closer to the enclosed world of *Scarface* or *Road to Glory* than to the far more open world of nature seen in films like *Red River* and *Hatari!* In that regard there *is* a sense of physical and social restriction at work in *His Girl Friday*. I believe it is a mistake, however, to see the film primarily in allegorical either/or terms—as if Hildy were being presented with two mutually exclusive alternatives between which she must choose, especially if the argument follows (as it often does) that Hildy is *forced* to choose Walter quite against her better judgment and instincts. I have already argued, in discussing *I Was a Male War Bride*, that Hildy's visit to the office of the *Morning Post* is evidence that she has *already* made her choice; she no more needs to confront Walter with the fact of her impending marriage than Henri needs to confront Catherine with her underwear in the later film. Note, furthermore, how effortlessly and immediately Hildy "fits"—via moving camera and point-of-view shots—into the space of the *Morning Post* city room, as if she really belongs there and knows it.

More importantly, it must be said that Hildy's conscious realization of her unconscious desire to stay with Walter and with the paper does not amount to a wholesale rejection of the values represented in the film by "innocents" like Earl, Bruce, Molly Malloy, and Mr. Pettibone. All are presented in sympathetic terms, and the ultimate effect of Walter's plan to win Hildy back is to save Earl Williams (or so we assume) and to expose the duplicity of the political machine of Sheriff Hartwell and the mayor. Burns, to be sure, is duplicitous after his own fashion, even going so far as to suborn the kidnapping of Hildy's future mother-in-law. But Walter's means, unlike the mayor's, never extend to murder, even though Walter may joke about it (the mayor is *not* joking when he orders the police to "shoot to kill"); and Walter's end, clearly, is to return Hildy to her marital and professional senses. And that's the point. For someone like Hildy, committed to language, to wit, and to a life of social action, marriage to Bruce Baldwin *would* be a kind of death, a denial of her essential self. But there are others, clearly, like Earl and Bruce, for whom middle-class routine offers meaning and purpose enough in life. Hildy's problem is that she feels compelled to live her life in traditional middle-class, home-and-baby terms; and the film's point is that Hildy must live life on her own professional and sexual terms if her life is to have real meaning.

Some women in Hawks, as we have seen, practice professions which are more typically practiced by men. Hildy Johnson, indeed, is

repeatedly referred to as a "newspaperman" and her presence in the
courthouse pressroom serves continually to challenge the notion that
women are only suited to be wives and mothers. Most of the more
independent female professionals in Hawks, however, are professional "women" in some sense for whom sexuality is an implicitly
important and largely positive element in the quest for a meaningful
existence.

Some of these women are gamblers whose professional success
depends in part on their sexual attractiveness. An early and clearly
negative example is Mary in *Barbary Coast*, who uses her beauty to
draw men to the crooked roulette wheel in the Bella Donna. A more
positive instance is evidenced by Tess in *Red River*. She shares with
Mary a certain measure of self-disgust (expressed in her angry initial
reaction to Matthew Garth)—but the emphasis in *Red River* is less on
Tess's duplicity (there really is none) than on her ability to "gamble"
on Dunson by asking him to take her along to Abilene; she even plays
with a deck of cards during the conversation. More positive yet is the
case of Feathers (Angie Dickinson) in *Rio Bravo*. Like Tess she is a
gambler, literally "throwing in" with John T. Chance (John Wayne)
when she tosses a flower pot through a window to distract Burdett's
men. But she demonstrates none of the self-disgust or self-doubt
which plagues Mary and Tess. She is, as she tells Chance, not that
"kind of girl."

The majority of the independent professional women in Hawks are
gamblers, however, only in a metaphoric sense; in practical terms
they tend more often to be or to become professional entertainers or
showgirls—like Bonnie Lee in *Only Angels Have Wings*, Sugarpuss
O'Shea in *Ball of Fire*, and Hollie MacGregor in *Red Line 7000*.
Theirs is a profession which is traditionally open to women; hence the
relative frequency of their presence in Hawks. But the showgirl
profession is also one which threatens to objectify them, to make
them nothing *but* women. Such is certainly the case with Tessie in *A
Girl in Every Port*, for instance. It is far more typical of the Hawksian
showgirl, however, to assert her human and sexual worth through or,
if necessary, in despite of her social role. Put another way, many
women in Hawks thrive in the entertainment or theatrical context.
They continue to be assertively and aggressively female; but the
assertion inevitably assumes the fact of sexual equality and it often has
the effect of foregrounding and therefore challenging codes of sexual
conduct which deny women their worth.

Twentieth Century (1934)

Most of the more genuinely independent Hawksian showgirls are found in the films after 1939. Those in the earlier films tend not so much to thrive as to suffer for playing the saloon-girl part. One clear exception to this rule exists, however, though it hardly seems adequate to describe the character of Lily Garland in *Twentieth Century* as a showgirl. As enacted by Carole Lombard she becomes rather a classic example of the witty, aggressive, self-possessed Hawksian woman whose assertion of personal worth is not only insistent but downright theatrical. She knows there are parts to play but insists upon equal billing.

There are two primary dangers in the world of *Twentieth Century:* (1) the danger, seen often in Hawks, of psychic and social rigidity (of roles which are too rigid or of roles which are played too rigidly) and (2) the danger of losing or not having an appreciative audience. The rigidity issue is first raised in the opening rehearsal scene. The play being rehearsed, for example, is a parable of sexual and social rigidity: Lily Garland (née Mildred Plotke) plays the role of Mary Jo Calhoun, whose Kentucky Colonel father promptly sends his daughter to her room and then shoots her young lover to death. Lily's problem in playing the part, furthermore, also involves an element of rigidity. She is clearly cowed by the situation, especially so when Oscar Jaffe (John Barrymore) takes over the rehearsal himself, and the only response which "Mary Jo" can muster up upon learning of her "lover's" death is a docile squeak. In Oscar Jaffe, however, Lily finds her proper audience. Wooden acting (Jaffe compares Lily to a nine-pin) and mousy squeaks are not good enough for Oscar Jaffe and he promptly undertakes a marathon rehearsal which, ironically but effectively, forces Lily out of her shell. Indeed, prior to Oscar's badgering Lily's gestures and expressions are restrained and conventional—but when she tells Oscar that she's "taken all the bullying [she's] gonna take" her body and voice gain both in flexibility (she literally rises up out of her chair to confront Jaffe) and self-expressiveness. As John Belton puts it, Lombard's "transformation into Lily Garland . . . marks the loss of a superficial identity but brings with it the realization of a new identity as actress that goes beyond the dull caricature existence and limited expressiveness of Mildred Plotke, the shop girl."[4] It is only by breaking with convention (the convention of female docility and reserve) that Lily gains the ability to "play with" conventions (of the sort embodied in *The Heart of Kentucky*).

In opposing Jaffe's single-mindedness Lily becomes an actress; Jaffe does not thereby become any less single-minded. Rather, like the father in *The Heart of Kentucky*, Jaffe keeps Lily a virtual prisoner in her art deco flat, threatening suicide one minute and violence the next (both threats seem more theatrical than real) in order to keep Lily as much to himself as possible, so that he is the only audience she has outside the theater. This by itself, however, may be understood in retrospect as a mark of the "Humpty Dumpty" love (as O'Malley terms it) which binds Oscar and Lily together; there is nothing to suggest that Jaffe ever treated any of his earlier discoveries in a similar manner. The problem is that their relationship is still cast largely in Svengali/Trilby, father/child terms (he calls her "child" throughout the rehearsal scene, for instance).

Lily's eventual departure for Hollywood, then, has the positive effect of permitting a realignment of their relationship on far more equal terms. Thus, after sneaking aboard the Twentieth Century Limited in Chicago (where his latest, Garlandless play has just folded), Oscar sheds his disguise as (and hence his identity as) the fatherly southern gentleman, and through the subsequent course of screwball events Jaffe repeatedly "sink[s] so low as to become an actor." Indeed, it is less out of fear for his life than from professional admiration (Jaffe fakes a death scene akin to that which Barrymore played in George Cukor's *Dinner at Eight*) that Lily—herself a passenger, as "second chance" would have it, on the Twentieth Century—finally consents to sign another contract with Jaffe. It is arguable, to be sure, that Lily's signing the contract represents a renewal of her subservience—especially so when Jaffe, at the rehearsal scene which closes the film, asks for chalk and begins once again to lay down tracks for Lily to follow. It is to be noted, though, that on the second runthrough Lily does not follow his direction, except to yell at him that he can't get away with it this time. Their relationship *began* with a scream, however, and there is something genuinely satisfying about the fact that Lily and Oscar are once again on screaming terms with one another.

Gentlemen Prefer Blondes (1953)

Gentlemen Prefer Blondes is arguably one of the most misunderstood and least appreciated of the later films of Howard Hawks. In the present context, moreover, it can clearly be seen as his penulti-

Twentieth Century: (top) Carole Lombard as Lily Garland; (bottom) John Barrymore as Oscar Jaffe, an "actor" at last.

mate "showgirl" film, with the emphasis equally on "show" and "girl." Therein, however, lies the problem: how are we to take the apparently upbeat aspect of the film's "show," its tone of full-throated garishness, of craziness and innocence somehow combined, when that show is clearly predicated to some degree on what the film itself portrays, however playfully, as a dehumanizing view of "girls"? Put another way, does the film celebrate or satirize the notion that "gentlemen prefer blondes"?[5]

The answer, I think, is both. Like many Hawks comedies, that is, *Gentlemen Prefer Blondes* works simultaneously at two levels, can be read simultaneously in two contexts. At one level, then, *Blondes* must be read exactly as a satire on the sexual values of patriarchal capitalism—though it is here that the film exhibits its primary (and to some, disquieting) ambiguity. The two showgirls at film's center, for instance, are clearly allied in their professionalism as entertainers (recall the coordinated movements and gestures of the film's marvelous opening number) and in their feelings for each other. But each takes a quite different stance relative to the issue of men and money.

For Marilyn Monroe's Lorelei Lee diamonds are indeed—as her song says—"a girl's best friend." Men for Lorelei are seen as a means to their acquisition (at one point the Charles Coburn character even "becomes" a diamond in Lorelei's eyes). For Jane Russell's Dorothy Shaw, however, men and money don't mix. She is put off when Eddie Malone (Elliott Reid) uses money (racehorses, specifically) as a come-on; is outraged to discover that she has fallen in love with a private detective out to get the goods on Lorelei's gold-digging; and is reconciled with Malone when he tells his boss, the father of Lorelei's "fiancé," to keep his money ("I resign"). Dorothy's concern for Lorelei, however, is completely consistent with the more humane values she embodies in her relationship with Malone. Put another way, Lorelei's gold-digging is adorable for Dorothy (and for us) on two accounts: (1) by playing the gold-digger role to the hilt Lorelei clearly exposes the class system which dictates the role (recall here the remarkable analogy Lorelei draws between beauty in women and money in men: even the patriarchal capitalist is impressed); and (2) Lorelei plays the role with a kind of childish enthusiasm which disallows the attribution of cynicism—hence the relationship she develops with young Henry Spofford III, who mirrors her odd combination of youth and age.

The satiric element of the film is thus directed at the gentlemen rather than the blondes. "Blondeness," as Dorothy demonstrates during the courtroom sequence, is a role which may be adopted or discarded—though sexual politics of the sort embodied by Mr. Esmond and Sir Francis "Piggy" Beekman clearly make the role seem obligatory and hence dehumanizing (recall the "faceless" women in Lorelei's solo dance number). What is most remarkable about *Gentlemen Prefer Blondes*, then, is the degree to which the women—both "blondes" at one point or another—refuse as far as possible to accept dehumanization. Indeed, it is precisely the ability of characters either to transcend or ignore what seem to be obligatory social roles that the film may be said to celebrate.

Transcendence of a sort is seen in the character of Lorelei generally, but especially during the film's centerpiece production number: "Diamonds Are a Girl's Best Friend." Particularly by contrast with the women who are frozen in place as stage props, Lorelei's incredible energy and idiosyncratic grace are strikingly self-expressive and independent. At one point, indeed, Lorelei is transfigured by a lighting change during which she seems to claim the entire stage for herself. More typically, though, the film's production numbers escape social obligation—the narrative obligation to maintain some measure of dramatic credibility, for instance—by ignoring ostensible motivation altogether. Thus Dorothy sings the "Bye, Bye Baby" number as if she were being left behind—despite the fact that she (and nearly everyone else involved) is leaving for Paris. Likewise, "Is There Anyone Here for Love?" is staged as an elaborate joke. Dorothy's sexual double entendres seem to fall on deaf ears while she sings. The members of the Olympic team are too busy working out to pay attention. But when the number concludes, the team members wind up with Dorothy in the swimming pool, their previously mechanical postures and stiff expressions giving way to smiles and laughter all around, as if the team had been in on the gag (as indeed it was) all along. The best example of this ability—on the part of both the characters and the film itself—to ignore convention is the "When Love Goes Wrong" number which begins as a lament but which becomes instead a classic Hawksian sing-along, spontaneous, social, and liberating.

The only possible exception to this pattern of expectations ignored or escaped is the reprise of "Two Little Girls from Little Rock" which concludes the film. Lorelei and Dorothy sing it while marching down the aisle to be married, Lorelei to the younger Mr. Esmond, Dorothy to Malone. Social and sexual conventions thus seem to be satisfied by the fact that the film concludes with a wedding. But the wedding ceremony is undercut in the mise-en-scène. Again we see Dorothy and Lorelei marching between ranks of onlookers, a repeated image in the film which is associated in most instances with the more grotesque aspects of sexuality. And when Dorothy and Lorelei get to the altar they are framed together in two shot: the grooms are off frame. By so doing Hawks clearly reinforces the degree to which the film celebrates the "Blondes" while satirizing the "Gentlemen." But the undercutting of sexual commitment implicit in the framing also has the effect of calling to mind the more negative aspects of marriage embodied in the relationship of Lord and Lady Beekman, who likewise are seldom seen together. The wedding ceremony can thus be seen as yet one more performance. This performance, however, transcends the terms of its presentation only at the cost of sexual commitment. In Hawks it is a high price to pay—and the apparent necessity for paying it may well account for the film's largely negative reputation.

Role Reversal/Role Consciousness

No concept is more central to Hawks criticism than the concept of role reversal. It can clearly be seen to underlie the commonly drawn distinction between the adventure films and the comedies. The two genres are aligned *against* each other, and the opposition is based largely on the reversal of sex roles—in the adventure films the men are dominant; in the comedies it's the women who run the show. I have already pointed to several deficiencies in this use of the role-reversal notion. Such reversals, it is commonly argued, are generally involuntary, are largely permanent, and are, in the comedies at least, essentially negative in their implications. In Chapter 3 I argue just the opposite: that role reversal in Hawks is often voluntary, transitory, and basically positive in its implications. Moreover, the present chapter raises serious doubts of another sort relative to the notion of role reversal. In the case of women, at least, the wholesale reversal of social roles simply does not happen in Hawks: women in his films continue to occupy roles which are traditionally considered female. Only in a very few instances—*His Girl Friday*, for example—do we see a woman play a traditionally masculine social role.

What matters most in Hawks is not so much role *reversal*, then, as role *consciousness*—an awareness of the necessity to distinguish personal worth from social role. Without such an awareness of the difference between *self* and *role*, reversal of any sort would be impossible. It is precisely for failing to make such a distinction, for example, that father figures in Hawks so often come to grief. In seeking to assert "the law" such characters inevitably impose overly rigid and therefore destructive role-definitions on others. In many cases the victims are women: Cesca is a "sister" in *Scarface*, Quita a "wife" in *Tiger Shark*, Bonnie a "chorus girl" in *Only Angels Have Wings*, etc. In other cases the victims are men. Thus Spike in *A Girl in Every Port* is locked into the "buddy" role vis-à-vis Bill, and his willingness to play that role to the exclusion of all others is clearly predicated on ignorance: he never learns the details of the previous relationship between Tessie and Bill. Thus Graham in *The Criminal Code* becomes a convict because Brady insists on playing the district-attorney role by the book. Thus Dunson in *Red River* is willing to kill to enforce the law implicit in the trail-drive contract. Indeed, it's because Dunson has too rigid a notion of Fen's social worth that he leaves her behind in the first place, thereby becoming, in some sense, his own victim.

Role consciousness and role flexibility in Hawks follow less from the wholesale reversal of social and sexual roles, then, than from the "foregrounding" of social/sexual codes. We have already discussed several important instances of this, as it is seen in those few films wherein women play male-typical roles but also and more strikingly in films like *Paid to Love*, *Twentieth Century*, and *Gentlemen Prefer Blondes* wherein central characters, especially women, are professional role players. Two other sorts of role foregrounding are worth commenting on briefly: (1) foregrounding through clothing, and (2) foregrounding through gesture or action.

No aspect of male/female role reversal in Hawks is more remarked upon than the occasional instances of cross-dressing, usually men wearing women's clothing. Indeed, it's the specter of men-become-women which critics seem to have in mind when discussing the theme of male humiliation in Hawksian comedy. To be accurate, it must be said that such cross-dressing scenes are both infrequent and brief in Hawks, most of them occurring in the Cary Grant comedies (*Bringing Up Baby*, *I Was a Male War Bride*, *Monkey Business*); and even in these films there is little sense that the goal of the woman is the emasculation of the male. Indeed, in *Baby* and *War Bride* men wear drag because the woman in each case wants to *encourage* the masculinity of the Cary Grant character. Only in *Monkey Business* is

Man-become-woman: Cary Grant in I Was a Male War Bride.

there a connection between the woman's sexual insecurity (under the influence of the youth drug Edwina shuts Barnaby out of their hotel room) and the man's adoption of female garb (Barnaby spends the night in the hotel laundry and comes out the next morning wearing a woman's coat). Accordingly, it seems inaccurate to read such sequences, and similar sequences in films like *War Bride* and *His Girl Friday* wherein women wear masculine clothes, trousers or man-cut suits, as reflecting exclusively on the matter of sexual confusion. Rather, I believe the primary emphasis in such instances (with *Bringing Up Baby* being only partially an exception) is to foreground the fact that clothing is socially and sexually coded—and arbitrarily so.

Gesture-play in general is another crucial element of the Hawksian style. Two kinds of gesture/action references are especially important relative to women and women's roles in Hawks: (1) sexually "coded" gestures, and (2) sexually "shared" gestures. Sexually "coded" gestures are frequent in Hawks—though it is typically the case that the coding is foregrounded by "gesture reversal." The most overt cases of this are moments of impromptu female impersonation wherein men, generally *not* in female dress, mimic female gestures. We see this, for example, in *Fig Leaves* (Eddie and Adam take turns playing "Eve" when Eddie instructs Adam on how to be a he-man husband—advice which Adam eventually rejects) and in *The Big Sky* (when a burly Quebecois ties a bandana around his head, hitches up his trousers, and dances on the cabin of the keel boat).

Another sexually coded gesture pattern in Hawks involves the habit of smoking—largely a male-typical habit until the 1940s. To be sure, it was not an exclusively male habit in the movies; but women who smoked on screen were generally marked as independent and rebellious by the gesture. The archetype here, clearly, is the Dietrich character in films like *Morocco* and *Shanghai Express*. But cigarette play in Hawks, usually associated with tough-minded women, can be traced back to Dolores in *Paid to Love* and to other early Hawksian females like Quita in *Tiger Shark* and Lee in *The Crowd Roars*. Indeed, when Mike Mascarenhas asks Quita to move in with him (and before it's clear that he is proposing marriage) she replies by asking whether he's "got a match?" One would not want to call this "male impersonation," not in the same sense that Eddie's "Eve" routine in *Fig Leaves* is "female impersonation" (which indicates the degree to which female gestures historically have been more strictly coded than male gestures)—but the gesture play in both cases depends upon and accordingly foregrounds the fact of sex-role expectations. Other

Hawks films wherein women appropriate male-typical gestures include *His Girl Friday* (Hildy opens an office gate for Walter), *Ball of Fire* (when Sugarpuss belts Miss Bragg with a wicked right cross), and *Man's Favorite Sport?* (Abbie pulls Roger's chair out from the table for him when they meet for dinner).

One final sort of gesture-play can be seen to contribute to the foregrounding or calling into question of sex-role expectations in Hawks—what I have termed sexually "shared" gestures. These are of two sorts. Some such gestures are shared across films. In *Only Angels Have Wings*, for instance, Jeff Carter prevents a fight between Kid Dabb and Bat McPherson by striking a match at the last minute: the pause created by the gesture allows Kid to regain control. We see an almost identical sequence in *To Have and Have Not*—but in the latter film it's the Lauren Bacall character who strikes the match, thereby preventing the Bogart character from losing control and punching out a double-dealing client. In both cases the gesture can be read as an instance of clear-headed improvisation, using a conventional action for unconventional purposes. Equally interesting in the second instance, however, is the degree to which the repetition of the gesture effectively asserts a relation of sexual parity: both the gesture and the intelligence it signifies are transferable across the sexes (and across films). Or consider the *Come and Get It* bar brawl sequence as an instance of a man and a woman sharing a gesture *within* a film. The brawl starts as a bottle and fist affair. But soon Lotta and Barney turn it into a marvelous game as they fling saucerlike serving trays back and forth through the space of the saloon. Again, improvisation is involved, and again its effect is to assert sexual equality: Lotta can fling trays just as well and just as joyfully as Barney Glasgow—and this despite her social role as a saloon girl.

Monogamy/Matrimony

"The interest of Hawks's work," according to Robin Wood, "derives from its ambiguous relationship to the dominant ideology."[6] And for Wood that ambiguity is almost entirely a matter of sex-role expectations, i.e., of heterosexuality and legalized monogamy, to both of which, argues Wood, Hawks seems only intermittently committed. I think Wood overstates the case for bisexuality in Hawks. There is a meaningful distinction to be drawn, it seems to me, between the portrayal of homosexual attraction and the questioning

Gesture play in (top) Only Angels Have Wings *and (bottom)* To Have and Have Not.

of overly rigid or overly codified sex-role definitions. Wood's observations on the status of marriage in Hawks, however, are of a different order. Put another way, considering the status of marriage in Hawks allows for some very interesting observations on the relationship between sexuality and society in the Hawksian cinema.

I have already demonstrated the degree to which women in Hawks tend to exist in ambiguous relationship to society and to social expectations: by and large they play "female" roles but almost always in terms which question or deny strict definitions of what those roles are worth or require. Put another way, we are always aware in Hawks of the woman *behind* the role.

Often that awareness depends upon our realization that the woman is oppressed by the role she plays, and in some few cases it's the "wife" role itself which is oppressive. In both *Trent's Last Case* and *Tiger Shark,* for instance, an older husband (Sigsbee Manderson/ Mike Mascarenhas) effectively denies the sexual integrity of his younger wife and attempts to murder her lover (the "murder" in *Trent's Last Case* is far more theatrical than in *Tiger Shark*: Manderson commits suicide but only after planting evidence intended to frame his wife's lover for the crime). In other films, marriage is shown to have both negative and positive implications. Thus, in *Fazil* marriage serves as a genuine expression of emotional commitment (and for both Fabienne and Fazil the marriage represents a break with habit or tradition), but it also leads to death when Fazil comes to insist that Fabienne play the marriage game by the Arab rules. In films like *His Girl Friday, Ball of Fire,* and *Man's Favorite Sport?* marriage alternatives are personified—quite clearly in the latter two films (Sugarpuss is torn between an English professor and a mobster in *Ball of Fire*; Roger Willoughby wavers between Abbie and Tex in *Man's Favorite Sport?*), more ambiguously in *His Girl Friday* (where Hildy's rejection of Bruce does not amount to a wholesale rejection of middle-class life).

Peter Wollen's assertion that "there is no married life" in Hawks is thus inaccurate in the extreme.[7] Indeed, largely positive marital relationships or their prospect are seen with remarkable frequency in his films: in *Fig Leaves* (Adam and Eve), *The Crowd Roars* (Spud, his wife, their child; Eddie and Anne), *Ceiling Zero* (Jake and Mary Lee), *Bringing Up Baby* (David and Susan), *Only Angels Have Wings* (Bat and Judy), *His Girl Friday* (Walter and Hildy), *Sergeant York* (Alvin and Gracie), *To Have and Have Not* (Paul and Helène de Bursac), *Red River* (Matt and Tess), *I Was a Male War Bride* (Henri and Catherine),

Monkey Business (Edwina and Barnaby), and *Hatari!* (Dallas and Sean). Accordingly, it must be said that high value is placed in Hawks on what are essentially monogamous sexual relationships.

Nevertheless, the ideological interest expressed by critics like Peter Wollen and Robin Wood is still quite valid—not because Hawks rejects monogamy but because monogamy in his films does not automatically or necessarily involve marriage. Positive sexual relationships are central, as we have seen, to the Hawksian vision. Indeed, positive sexual relationships are essential to civilization in Hawks: witness *Barbary Coast, To Have and Have Not,* and *Red River.* Matrimony, however, is not essential. Men and women will often express commitment to one another in Hawks—but without expressing it in the language of marriage. Thus in *Twentieth Century* the language of love is the language of the theater. Denet and Monique confess their love for each other to Laroche in *Road to Glory*—but no mention is made of marriage. In *Only Angels Have Wings* Jeff does not ask Bonnie to marry him: the question is whether or not she will "stay"—as it is relative to Cole Thornton in *El Dorado.* In *The Big Sleep,* likewise, sexual commitment is explicit ("I guess I'm in love with you") but the issue of marriage between Marlowe and Vivian is not raised. Especially interesting in this regard is *Red Line 7000*: sexual commitments are central to the movie ("loving" and "staying" are key words throughout), but not one of the three couples in the film has any plans to be married.

This focus in Hawks on the importance of sexual commitments does not accord very well with the standard view of the films, in which male/female relationships are almost always seen as a matter of one sex dominating the other—hence the fact, perhaps, that critics (male critics especially) have tended not to notice the incredible variety and frequency of sexual pairings in Hawks. And to the extent that such an emphasis on the importance of heterosexual relationships is consistent with the sexual ideology of Hollywood generally Hawks is quite properly described as a "classical" Hollywood filmmaker. It can also be said, however, that Hawks never *equates* sexual commitment with legal or social fact: "the law" can never guarantee love in Hawks. Indeed, sexuality as a fact seems *prior to* society as a set of conventions in Hawks, conventions which are repeatedly foregrounded or questioned in the films. Marriage is thus presented in Hawks as one option among several. The absence of marriage in a particular instance, therefore, ought not to be read as an attack on the fact of heterosexuality. Indeed, Hawks is one of Hollywood's most thoroughly "heterosexual" directors in the sense that his films evidence an abiding concern for male/female relationships. What sets Hawks apart from his Hollywood contemporaries is his willingness to loosen up or to question the terms wherein those relationships find expression. Perhaps this accounts for the incredible "aliveness" so often found in Hawksian couples: men and women in Hawks must rely upon themselves, upon their own sense of felt life, and not on social conventions, to validate the integrity of their relationships.

6

Some Aspects of *Rio Bravo*

"ALL INQUIRY," WRITES E. D. HIRSCH, "is a process directed toward increasing the probability of learning the truth."[1] An important step in any such process is the testing of accepted paradigms. My task in this book, accordingly, has been two-fold: (1) to locate those areas of anomaly where the data of the films are demonstrably ill-accounted for when read according to the standard hypotheses; and (2) to propose a new set of hypotheses which offer the promise of a better "fit" between thematic generalities and stylistic specifics.

Wherever possible I have focused on the latter aspect of this two-fold critical task. This explains my decision to discuss a good many films, most of them from the twenties and thirties, which have hitherto been largely ignored. Most Hawks criticism to date has focused primarily on the films made after 1937. Discussing the earlier films thus provides an opportunity to expand the canon. Doing so also makes it possible to test the standard viewpoint without becoming overly embroiled in negative arguments. (No attempt has been made to duck the issues here. If anything, the standard view of Hawks is more strongly urged in terms of the earlier films which I focus on rather than the later ones.) As a consequence, however, it has also been necessary to slight a good many films which have previously been considered obligatory in discussions of Hawks. That neglect is regrettable—but only to the extent that it makes my general argument somewhat more tentative. However, given the fact that art works are characterized by their "inexhaustibility," which allows our sense of a text to grow as new connotations occur to us or are pointed out, certitude in such matters will always be elusive.[2] I will account this essay a success if it demonstrates the possibility of reading the films of Howard Hawks well and attentively—but from a different

vantage point, within a different framework from the one proposed by
Peter Wollen and others. That's task enough for one book.

Ideally, then, the job of this final chapter would be to summarize
my approach to Hawks and to test it at length against that Hawks film
whose treatment is considered most obligatory in any evaluation of
his oeuvre: *Rio Bravo*. Formal limitations of this series prevent that.
An extended reading of *Rio Bravo* being impossible, I have chosen to
indicate those features of the film which take on new or added interest
when read in the context of the present discussion.

I. The generic status of *Rio Bravo* is exceedingly problematic.

For most Hawks scholars *Rio Bravo* is a remarkably "typical"
movie. In the words of Robin Wood, "*Rio Bravo* is the most traditional of films. The whole of Hawks is immediately behind it, and
the whole tradition of the western."[3] Neither of these latter two
assertions is well grounded.

The notion that *Rio Bravo* is a typical or traditional Western has not
been well argued—not even by Robin Wood. Indeed, in *Six Guns
and Society* Will Wright has suggested that *Rio Bravo* marks an
important *break* with the tradition of the classical Western. It is, he
says, the earliest example of the "Professional Plot" in which "the
symbolic emphasis is no longer on the relationship of the hero to
society but on the relationships of the heroes among themselves."[4] I
will return to this point.

More importantly, I would argue that *Rio Bravo* is a remarkably
atypical Hawks film in certain crucial and thematically important
respects. Both Wood and Kathleen Murphy, for example, follow the
standard model in describing the film as "a summing-up of Hawks's
adventure films" wherein "Hawks strips everything down to a basic
stoic principle" (Wood, 52, 50). The film's "social background is kept
to the barest minimum" (Wood, 37), thus creating "a cinematic world
in which Hawksian metaphysics are played out practically *ab
nihilo*."[5] In outline, indeed, *Rio Bravo* comes closer than any other
single film, except *Only Angels Have Wings*, to enacting the prototypical Hawksian fable of male elitism preserved against the threats
of a hostile universe and fast-talking women. It is precisely this view
of Hawks which I have rejected in this book. To be typical in Wollenesque terms is thus to be remarkably *a*typical in terms of the
model which I have proposed here.

Rio Bravo is also atypical in certain stylistic respects. Central to the
Hawksian cinema is a constant interplay between action and iconog-

raphy. Both *Scarface* and *Red River,* for instance, place considerable emphasis on the contrast between the self-centeredness of characters and the self-consciousness of the film's narration. Characters like Tony Camonte are too caught up in their own plans and desires to acknowledge the existence of a world outside themselves—a world, however, which the films acknowledge precisely by means of genre and director references, to Von Sternberg, to Ford, to Capra, etc. What is striking about *Rio Bravo,* then, is the almost total *lack* of such references. True enough, *Rio Bravo* begins with an homage to Von Sternberg's *Underworld* (the action in both films is initiated when a drunk is tempted to fish money from a spittoon) but the generic coordinates thereafter are drawn almost entirely from *within* the Hawksian canon—and especially, as critics have repeatedly pointed out, from *Only Angels Have Wings* and *To Have and Have Not.*[6] Even the *Underworld* reference, however, can be read as a turning inward: Hawks has frequently claimed to have collaborated with Ben Hecht on the *Underworld* scenario.[7]

Rio Bravo, then, like many of the films which follow it in the canon, is decidedly introspective in tone: it is arguable that introspection is one of its primary thematic concerns—both for the character of Dude (Dean Martin), whose introspection takes the form of drunkenness, and for Chance (John Wayne), whose introspection is expressed most strikingly in his hostility toward Feathers (Angie Dickinson). It is worth remarking that the solution, in both cases, involves a "watcher"—someone whose concerned attention makes it impossible for the self-centered character to lose contact altogether with a world beyond the self. Thus Chance "watches" Dude, Feathers "watches" Chance (standing watch outside his bedroom with a shotgun in her lap, for instance)—and, perhaps, we "watch" *Rio Bravo,* our concerned attention helping it to be a better film as Chance's helps Dude to be a better person.

II. The thematic value of the John Wayne character in *Rio Bravo* is also problematic.

For most critics Sheriff John T. Chance is "morally infallible." "As the concrete embodiment of the Hawksian values," writes Robin Wood, Chance "is the nucleus round which the others organize themselves, without which there would be no possibility of order" (56). Such a reading of Chance's character is perfectly in accord with genre expectations (Western sheriffs are traditionally seen as figures of law and order)—but it also accords with the standard view of

Hawks's adventure films: as leader of the Hawksian group Chance may be read as embodying exactly those values of comradeship and professionalism which such groups are typically seen as representing.

I have already suggested that *Rio Bravo* cannot be (or has not been) well read as a traditional Western. I would also suggest that the thematic function of the Chance character in *Rio Bravo* is diminished when measured, as it often is, against the standard picture of Hawksian professionalism. Put another way, in the terms of the present discussion it is a major anomaly that Chance should be presented as an embodiment of "the law." Such characters in Hawks—Brady in *The Criminal Code*, Jeff in *Only Angels Have Wings,* Dunson in *Red River*—are inevitably called into question by their willingness to enforce the law, especially when their enforcement of it so frequently involves an explicit denial of sexuality. *Rio Bravo* would be atypical indeed if Chance were totally faultless. He isn't.

It is not just a matter, as Robin Wood describes it, of Chance's "limitations"—of his inability to participate in the Dude/Colorado/Stumpy sing-along or to "establish authority" over Feathers (52–54). It is rather the case that Chance's initial treatment of Feathers is quite explicitly dehumanizing and wrong-headed, based on just the same sort of false sexual stereotypes which allow Jeff Carter to brand Bonnie Lee a "chorus girl" in *Only Angels Have Wings*. More specifically, Chance assumes, on the basis of a handbill and a shorted poker deck, that Feathers is cheating at cards—despite the fact that she was not the only stranger in the card game. To be sure, upon confronting Feathers in her room Chance quite properly points out that the other (male) stranger is still downstairs at the table—but Chance orders Feathers to leave town without ever checking to see if she has the shorted cards up her sleeve. Feathers gives him the opportunity to search her—but Chance declines. As Feathers puts it to Chance: "I think you're embarrassed"—to which Colorado (Ricky Nelson) adds that Chance sure "ought to be." It's the man downstairs who's been cheating. It all adds up. Chance, as Carlos (the hotel-keeper) points out, does "not know women," assumes they are all "no good," just like the one who made a drunk out of Dude, and hence Chance treats Feathers like a stagecoach girl from the moment he sets eyes on her, *before* he ever observes her playing cards or sees the incriminating handbill.

Crucial to any reading of *Rio Bravo* is an understanding of the connection between its romantic plot (the relationship between

Chance and Feathers) and its adventure plot (involving the arrest of
Joe Burdett and the attempt by Chance and his deputies to hold Joe in
custody, despite his brother Nathan's desire to break him out). For
Robin Wood the connection is thematic: Chance and Feathers are
variations on the theme of self-respect, while the Burdett brothers
serve to parody the theme, in that neither is worthy of respect.
Considering Chance as a Hawksian father figure (Dude even calls him
"Papa" at one point) suggests a different reading of the relationship
between the film's two primary plots. Briefly, we can say that the
issue in both plots is precisely the denial of the reality of the world
outside the self—either by seeking to impose dehumanizing
stereotypes on others (Joe Burdett tempts Dude to fish the coin from
the spittoon; Chance orders Feathers out of town) or by denying the
humanness of others altogether through the act of murder, as Joe
Burdett kills the man who tries to prevent Joe from working Dude
over.

The ambiguity of the Chance character is thus a function of the fact
that he plays a central role in both plot-threads. In the adventure plot
he is a victim of Nathan Burdett's ability to shut down the town,
cutting it off from the world outside. As Chance puts it to Pat Wheeler
(Ward Bond), Burdett has the town "so bottled up" that Chance "can't
get Joe out or any help in." In the romantic plot, however, Chance is
guilty of a related transgression for denying Feathers the right to be
herself; more specifically, in ordering her out of town he denies her
the right to gamble in public. Chance's transgression, however, is *not*
predicated on a callous disregard for human life of the sort which
motivates the Burdetts. Witness the concern Chance shows for
Dude, or Chance's anger at the killing of Pat Wheeler. Rather, like
Jeff Carter in *Only Angels Have Wings,* Chance's surface tendency to
trivialize sexual relationships is evidence that at a deeper level he
takes such relationships seriously. He *is* embarrassed by his treatment of Feathers, and Chance's embarrassment justifies her growing
affection and respect. If anything, in experiencing the isolation imposed by Nathan Burdett (in being "bottled up"—like Dude) Chance
receives an education in the art of acknowledging and relying upon
others, despite his immediate estimations of their worth or skills.
Thus by film's conclusion Chance receives unexpected assistance
from Dude, from Colorado, from Feathers, from Carlos, and from
Stumpy. Dude's transformation from drunk to deputy is not the only
transformation in the film.

III. Hostility in the world of *Rio Bravo*
is a function of human agents.

Underlying the Hawks-as-stoic argument is an implicit assumption that the Hawksian universe is essentially hostile: hence all the talk about "chaos" and "darkness" and "absurdity." Evidence for this view of the Hawksian cosmos is hard to come by, however. Even in *Only Angels Have Wings*—one of the few Hawks films wherein nature (the birds, the fog) plays any part in determining the course or outcome of the action—the primary source of hostility is not nature itself so much as man's (Jeff's) distrust of it. A similar situation obtains in *Rio Bravo*.

"Nature" as such plays no direct role in the "adventure" plot of *Rio Bravo*. Rather, hostility attends primarily upon the actions of human agents. This is obviously so in the case of the Burdett brothers: Joe kills a man in the opening sequence, and Nathan's hired guns threaten murder (and do kill Pat Wheeler) throughout the film. Less obvious but equally interesting is the case of John T. Chance. One could argue, indeed, that it is Chance's hostility—especially his hostility toward women—which initiates the violence in *Rio Bravo*.

It is commonly assumed, for instance, that Chance was accurate when he told Dude that Dude's stagecoach girl was "no good." Indeed, Dude eventually declares, though jokingly, that Chance was "right" about her. Might it not have been the case, however, that Chance was *wrong* about Dude's girl, as wrong about her as he is initially about Feathers? Might not Chance's enmity, then, have been the *cause* of Dude's leaving town—or even of Dude's subsequent inability to sustain his relationship with the woman? As Dunson in *Red River* it was John Wayne who wrongly rejected Fen and turned thereafter to drink: Dude's situation in *Rio Bravo* is strikingly similar. Likewise, we are entitled to wonder at the way in which Chance humiliates Dude by kicking the spittoon in the film's opening scene. It is not that he shouldn't have intervened. But the method of his intervention is charged with an unnecessary measure of disgust and self-righteousness. Indeed, the shot/reverse-shot cutting of the sequence invites us to compare Chance with Joe Burdett: both occupy a similar position relative to Dude. And clearly it is Chance's action which initiates the violence by changing the tempo of the scene: Chance kicks the spittoon, Dude in his anger retaliates against Chance and then goes for Joe, Joe proceeds to work Dude over, the stranger intervenes, and Joe plugs him.

Furthermore, the contention that the world of *Rio Bravo* (and of Hawks generally) is essentially hostile ignores the quite obvious fact

Two camera angles during the shot/reverse shot cutting on the spittoon sequence in Rio Bravo.

that his characters are usually much the better for their experiences. As elsewhere in Hawks, the major characters in *Rio Bravo* are repeatedly granted "second chances" which enable them to overcome or undo their previous mistakes. This is especially evident in the relationship of Chance, Dude, and Feathers. Feathers gets a second chance at love by falling in love with Chance. More importantly, like many a Hawksian woman, Feathers is herself an agent of a benevolent universe: she represents a "second chance" both for Dude and for John T. This is literally true when Feathers helps Colorado to prevent Burdett's men from taking Chance prisoner (not only is Chance's life at stake but also Dude's recovery). More significantly, the arrival of Feathers on the stagecoach gives Chance an opportunity to understand how wrong he was (or might have been) the first time. And there is a clear parallel between Chance's changing attitude toward Feathers and Dude's redemption from drink. It's as if Chance's acceptance of Feathers were crucial in helping Dude regain his self-respect by demonstrating that women (and life) are indeed trustworthy.

IV. Meaning in *Rio Bravo* is not asserted despite the world but is found within it.

The notion that the Hawksian universe is essentially hostile has a corollary: that characters do not *find* meaning in life but rather *assert* meaning despite the essential "absurdity" of existence. At its most sophisticated, the argument draws upon the language of Hemingway criticism: Hawksian heroes are "code heroes" who employ their professional and linguistic skills to "impose meaning upon otherwise senseless event and circumstance" (Murphy, 314). The premise that events and circumstances in Hawks are "senseless" is highly questionable. There is a clear logic to the hostility found in the world of the films: hostility derives almost entirely from human beings and actions. The world itself, by contrast, is essentially benevolent— especially if characters can overcome their fears of existence and get in tune with the natural rhythms of time and sexuality. However, the idea that Hawks's characters are "semantically skillful" remains interesting nevertheless, especially for the light it casts upon the relationship of characters to their social environment in Hawks.

It is frequently noted, for example, that Hawks's characters speak a sort of "Hawksian English." They "know talk is important: they talk about it all the time."[8] Indeed, *Rio Bravo*, as Richard Jameson has

demonstrated, is one of the "talkiest" pictures in the Hawks canon—
especially as that talk serves to explore and define the concept of
"good"-ness (see Jameson and Murphy for details). But to say that the
characters in *Rio Bravo* are attuned to the subtleties of conversation is
not to say that they *create* meaning apart from or in defiance of the
world. Rather, their ability to converse at all is evidence of their
dependency on the world outside themselves—on a world of language and language users. In fact, the richness of connotation and
association in *Rio Bravo* (and in Hawks generally) depends not only
upon language itself but also upon a sensitivity to its social context.
It's for lack of that sensitivity that Pat Wheeler is killed, for instance,
and a similar lack of sensitivity is implicit in Chance's attempt to deny
sexuality by treating Feathers as a "no good" stagecoach girl. Indeed,
Chance is wrong here precisely for attempting to *impose* meaning on
the world (on Feathers) rather than allow the world to be meaningful
in its own terms.

One of the more striking visual features of *Rio Bravo* bears upon
this issue of the relationship of character to environment: Hawks's use
of costume and color. Briefly put—the visual environment of *Rio
Bravo* is dominated by solid and relatively muted colors: the light
blue sky, the tan colored dirt streets and adobe buildings, the darker
woodwork of the hotel and the dark brown walls of the jail. Likewise,
the costumes of Chance and his deputies are also made up of relatively solid blocks of color—orange/red or blue shirts, dark or tan
colored leather vests, brown or tan (and well-worn) cowboy hats. By
contrast, Joe Burdett is introduced wearing a brightly colored hide
vest and a large, store-perfect black hat—and Nathan's men, as a
group, are given to shirts of wide checks or plaids and to large and
idiosyncratic headgear. It is not a matter of an absolute distinction
between Chance's crew and Burdett's: there is an interesting interplay, for example, between the outfits worn by Joe Burdett and
Dude, especially after Dude gets cleaned up and puts on his own
good clothes. But it is clear that Chance and his men "fit" into the
visual world they inhabit far more readily than Burdett's men. Again,
it's a question of accepting one's place *in* the universe rather than
asserting one's identity over and against it.

Of course, it is possible to fit too readily (or too rigidly) into the
world. Chance's problem in *Rio Bravo*, for instance, is less a matter of
asserting meaning over and against the world than of withdrawing too
thoroughly into a specific corner of it. This is true in a literal, physical
sense. Chance and his deputies spend much of their time inside the

jail, and they eventually decide to hole up there until the U. S. marshal can arrive to take custody of Joe Burdett—but circumstances (benevolently, as it turns out) force Chance and company to leave the safety of the lock-up and to face Burdett and his gang out in the open. Indeed, being out in the open allows others (Stumpy, Carlos) to come to the aid of Chance and Colorado—and it also allows for improvisations (Dude tackles Joe Burdett when the time comes to exchange prisoners, for instance) of the sort which so frequently enable Hawksian characters to turn calamity into celebration: hence *Rio Bravo's* famous "turkey shoot" sequence in which Stumpy throws the dynamite toward Burdett's warehouse while Chance and Dude take turns detonating the explosives with gunfire.

In metaphoric terms, furthermore, this physical movement outward is paralleled by an emotional movement on the part of John T. Chance. At the beginning of the film he is locked into his role as sheriff—and his enforcement of the law involves an implicit denial of sexuality. By film's conclusion, however, Chance has learned to play the sheriff role—to "play with" the role—in far less dehumanizing terms. His final "official" act is to threaten the arrest of Feathers for indecent exposure if she wears a revealing stage-costume in public—which Feathers interprets as an expression of affection ("I thought you were never going to say . . . that you loved me")—but his final gesture is to toss the offending tights *out* the window, to the street below, as if to acknowledge publicly the sexual component of life which he had earlier denied. Given the fact that Chance's attitude toward women may very well have "initiated" the film's action, this reconciliation of male and female represents an altogether appropriate and characteristically satisfying conclusion.

V. A final note on genre.

Earlier I cited Will Wright to the effect that *Rio Bravo* is an atypical western—and I went on to suggest that *Rio Bravo* is also a somewhat atypical Hawks film. Both assertions, it can be seen, depend upon the degree to which the film's central characters are read as existing *apart from* society. Clearly, however, the thematic progress of *Rio Bravo* is precisely in the opposite direction—toward demonstrating the necessity of existing *within* society and *within* the world of nature and time. The atypicality of *Rio Bravo* can be understood in retrospect, then, as a matter of degree rather than kind. *Rio Bravo* is *less* explicit than other Hawks Westerns (and other Westerns generally) in assert-

Reconciling male and female: John Wayne as John T. Chance and Angie Dickinson as Feathers in Rio Bravo.

ing the identity of personal and social concerns: compare it in this regard to *Red River* and *Rio Lobo*—the action in both films is set quite explicitly against the social background provided by the Civil War. Ultimately, however, the values celebrated in *Rio Bravo*—of wit, intelligence, and sexuality: social values all—*are* consistent with those celebrated in other films by Howard Hawks. It's just that those values are put at far greater hazard in *Rio Bravo* than elsewhere. Perhaps that helps to account for the intensity of response which the film continues to evoke. *Rio Bravo* may not "justify the existence of Hollywood" by itself—but the complexity of its thematic structure more than justifies a willingness to say so.

Notes and References

Preface

1. Monroe Beardsley, *Aesthetics: Problems in the Philosophy of Criticism* (New York: Harcourt, Brace & World, 1958), p. 539. On the applicability of Beardsley to film criticism see William Cadbury, "Human Experience and the Work Itself," *Journal of the University Film Association* 29, no. 1 (1977):25–32.

2. C. S. Lewis, *An Experiment in Criticism* (Cambridge: Cambridge University Press, 1961), p. 137.

3. See William Cadbury, "Auteurism: Theory as against Policy," *Cinemonkey* 5, no. 1 (1979):35–40. See also Leland A. Poague, "Explicating the Obvious: Five Propositions on the Problem of Value in Literary Studies," *Journal of Aesthetic Education* 11, no. 4 (1977):35–43.

4. See Raymond Durgnat, "Hawks Isn't Good Enough," *Film Comment* 13, no. 4 (1977):8–19.

Chapter One

1. Peter Wollen, *Signs and Meaning in the Cinema* (Bloomington, Ind., 1969; 2nd ed., 1972). Wollen's chapter on the auteur theory has been reprinted in Bill Nichols, ed., *Movies and Methods* (Berkeley: University of California Press, 1976), pp. 529–42, and in Gerald Mast and Marshall Cohen, eds., *Film Theory and Criticism,* 2nd ed. (New York: Oxford University Press, 1979), pp. 680–91. Wollen's chapter also appeared in the first edition of Mast and Cohen (1974).

2. See, for instance, the discussions of Hawks in Leo Braudy's *The World in a Frame* (Garden City, N.Y.: Anchor Press/Doubleday, 1976), and William Luhr and Peter Lehman's *Authorship and Narrative in the Cinema* (New York: G. P. Putnam's Sons, 1977).

3. Jacques Rivette's "Génie de Howard Hawks" first appeared in *Cahiers du Cinéma,* no. 23 (May 1953); references in the text will be to the translation published in Joseph McBride, ed., *Focus on Howard Hawks* (Englewood Cliffs, N.J., 1972), pp. 70–77. Andrew Sarris's "The World of Howard Hawks" appeared initially in *Films and Filming* 8, no. 10 (July 1962)

and no. 11 (August 1962); references in the text will be to the McBride anthology. Citations of Peter Bogdanovich, *The Cinema of Howard Hawks* (New York, 1962) and Robin Wood, *Howard Hawks* (Garden City, N.Y., 1968) will refer to the original editions.

4. François Truffaut's essay first appeared in *Cahiers du Cinéma*, no. 31; an English translation, "A Certain Tendency of the French Cinema," is reprinted in Nichols, ed., *Movies and Methods* (cited above), pp. 224–37. The Hawks interview by Becker, Rivette, and Truffaut is reprinted (in translation) in Andrew Sarris, *Interviews with Film Directors* (New York: Bobbs-Merrill, 1967; rpt. New York: Avon, 1969), pp. 228–40.

5. The Hawks pieces in *Movie*, no. 5 are as follows (see bibliography for additional information): unsigned introduction (p. 7), the Bogdanovich interview (pp. 8–18), "Rivette on Hawks" (pp. 19–20), Perkins on Hawks's "Comedies" (pp. 21–22), Shivas on "Blondes" (pp. 23–24), Wood on *Rio Bravo* (pp. 25–27), Perkins on *Hatari!* (pp. 28–30), Hawks filmography (pp. 31–34).

6. Robin Wood, "Responsibilities of a Gay Film Critic," *Film Comment* 14, no. 1 (1978):12–17.

7. Robin Wood, *Personal Views* (London, 1976), pp. 190–206 ("Hawks De-Wollenized").

Chapter Two

1. Wood, *Personal Views*, pp. 190–206.

2. I make this point in the conclusion of *The Cinema of Ernst Lubitsch* (New York: A. S. Barnes & Co., 1978).

3. Kathleen Murphy, "Howard Hawks: An American Auteur in the Hemingway Tradition," (Ph.D. diss., University of Washington, 1977), p. 188ff.

4. Alan Williams, "Narrative Patterns in 'Only Angels Have Wings,'" *Quarterly Review of Film Studies* 1, no. 4 (1976):357–72.

5. Wood, *Howard Hawks*, p. 17.

6. John Belton, *The Hollywood Professionals, Vol. 3* (New York, 1974), p. 9. See Peter Hogue, "How It Is," *Movietone News*, no. 40 (1975), pp. 1–7, for a "darker" view of the comedy in *Only Angels*.

7. John Belton, "I Was a Male War Bride," *Velvet Light Trap*, no. 3 (1971), p. 26.

8. Wood, *Howard Hawks*, pp. 84–85.

Chapter Three

1. Molly Haskell, "Howard Hawks: Masculine Feminine," *Film Comment* 10, no. 2 (1974):35.

2. Jeffrey Richards, "The Silent Films of Howard Hawks," *Focus on Film*, no. 25 (1976), p. 25.

3. Bogdanovich, p. 8.

4. Kenneth W. Munden, ed., *The American Film Institute Catalog* (New York: R. R. Bowker, 1971), pp. 626, 813.

5. Jean Gili, *Howard Hawks* (Paris, 1971), pp. 31–36.

6. See Donald C. Willis, *The Films of Howard Hawks* (Metuchen, N.J., 1975), pp. 102–104.

Chapter Four

1. Andrew Sarris, "The World of Howard Hawks," in Joseph McBride, ed., *Focus on Howard Hawks*, p. 41.

2. Wood, *Howard Hawks*, p. 62.

3. Murphy, pp. 56, 58, 62.

4. John Belton, "Scarface," *Bright Lights* 1, no. 4 (1976):21.

5. Bruce Kawin, *Faulkner and Film* (New York, 1977), pp. 89–90.

6. Mitchell Cohen, "Hawks in the 30s," *Take One* 4, no. 12 (1975):10.

7. Robin Wood, "Part Two: Who the Hell is Howard Hawks?" *Focus!*, no. 2 (1967), p. 8; Wood, *Howard Hawks*, p. 124.

8. Robert Sklar, "Empire to the West: Red River," in John E. O'Connor and Martin A. Jackson, eds., *American History/American Film* (New York: Frederick Ungar Publishing, 1979), p. 169. See also Durgnat, pp. 8–19, and Donald F. Larsson, "The Formal Structure of Red River and the 'Hawksian Woman,'" *Heritage of the Great Plains* 8, no. 1 (1980):1–7.

9. Similar use is made of voice-over narration in *The Big Sky* and *Land of the Pharaohs*.

Chapter Five

1. Naomi Wise, "The Hawksian Woman," *Take One* 3, no. 3 (1972):18; see also Leigh Brackett, "A Comment on the Hawksian Woman," *Take One* 3, no. 6 (1972):19–20.

2. Marilyn Campbell, "His Girl Friday: Production for Use," *Wide Angle* 1, no. 2 (1976):25. See also Tom Powers, "His Girl Friday: Screwball Liberation," *Jumpcut*, no. 17 (1978), pp. 25–27, and David Bordwell and Kristin Thompson, "His Girl Friday," in *Film Art* (Reading, Mass.: Addison-Wesley, 1979), pp. 234–39.

3. Wood, *Howard Hawks*, p. 77.

4. Belton, *The Hollywood Professionals, Vol. 3*, p. 24.

5. See Maureen Turim, "Gentlemen Consume Blondes," *Wide Angle* 1, no. 1 (Revised and Expanded, 1979):52–59.

6. Robin Wood, "Hawks: Retrospect, 1978," unpublished manuscript, p. 4. See also "Responsibilities of a Gay Film Critic," pp. 12–17.

7. Wollen, p. 88.

Chapter Six

1. E. D. Hirsch, Jr., *The Aims of Interpretation* (Chicago: University of Chicago Press, 1976), p. 151.

2. See William Cadbury, "Semiology, Human Nature, and John Ford," *Cinemonkey* 5, no. 2 (1979):40.

3. Wood, *Howard Hawks*, p. 35.

4.   Will Wright, *Six Guns and Society* (Berkeley: University of California Press, 1975), p. 87.

5.   Murphy, p. 309.

6.   See Wood, *Howard Hawks,* but also William Luhr, "Howard Hawks: Hawksthief," *Wide Angle* 1, no. 2 (1976):10–20, and John Fell, "Vladimir Propp in Hollywood," *Film Quarterly* 30, no. 3 (1977):19–28.

7.   See "Hawks Talks," an interview with Hawks by Joseph McBride and Gerald Peary, *Film Comment* 10, no. 3 (1974):51.

8.   Richard T. Jameson, "Talking & Doing in Rio Bravo," *Velvet Light Trap,* no. 12 (1974), p. 28.

Selected Bibliography

The bibliographic entries which follow have been selected in accord with the following criteria: (1) to represent the major trends in Hawks criticism, (2) to guide readers to articles or essays on films which I have *not* discussed in detail, and (3) to acknowledge those authors or articles which have had especial influence on my own approach to Hawks. I have made no attempt to be exhaustive. Articles cited in the Notes and References, for example, are listed here *only* if they are of special historical interest in the development of Hawks scholarship. Likewise, where an article or essay has been reprinted I only cite the most readily available source, except in cases where the date and place of original publication are of genuine historical significance. Further references may be found in Gili, McBride, and Murphy (below). A final note: the bulk of Hawks scholarship has appeared in periodicals or as chapter-length discussions in books. It seems to me, accordingly, that the most accurate and useful picture of the criticism results if all entries, books and periodicals alike, are listed by author without further categorization.

Bellour, Raymond. "The Obvious and the Code." *Screen* 15, no. 4 (Winter 1974/1975):7–17. Bellour describes his remarks on *The Big Sleep* as an "analytical description of twelve shots isolated from a film which can justifiably figure as one of the models of American high classicism."

Belton, John. "Monkey Business." *Film Heritage* 6 (Winter 1970/1971):19–26. It is typical of Belton to extend thematic analysis (drawn here quite openly from Wood) into the realm of visual style. This early Belton effort is less successful in this regard than much of his later work.

———. "Hawks and Co." In *Focus on Howard Hawks*. Edited by Joseph McBride. Englewood Cliffs, N.J.: Prentice-Hall, 1972, pp. 94–108. This piece originally appeared in *Cinema* (U.K.), No. 9 (1971). Its discussion of *Only Angels Have Wings* was reprinted in *The Hollywood Professionals, Vol. 3* (see below). It is primarily of interest now for Belton's extended remarks on *Tiger Shark*.

———. "I Was a Male War Bride." *Velvet Light Trap*, no. 3 (Winter 1971/1972), pp. 26–29. Clearly the finest of Belton's several fine pieces on Hawks.

————. "John Wayne: As Sure as the Turning O' the Earth." *Velvet Light Trap*, no. 7 (Winter 1972/1973), pp. 25–28. Belton discusses the Wayne "persona" as it developed in *Red River* and *She Wore a Yellow Ribbon*.

————. *The Hollywood Professionals, Vol. 3: Howard Hawks, Frank Borzage, Edgar G. Ulmer*. New York: A. S. Barnes & Co., 1974. Belton discusses *The Dawn Patrol, Scarface, Twentieth Century, His Girl Friday, Only Angels Have Wings, Red River, Rio Bravo, Hatari!, El Dorado*, and *Rio Lobo*.

————. "Scarface." *Bright Lights* 1, No. 4 (Summer 1976):19–21. A discussion of the film's production history with additional comments on film-style in *Scarface*.

————. Letter on *Red River*. *Movietone News*, no. 52 (October 1976), pp. 24–25. Belton discusses the differences between the original-release version of *Red River*, which has a voice-over narration spoken by Walter Brennan, and the prerelease "book" version, wherein the narrative function is assigned to shots of the diary kept by Groot. See also remarks by Gregg Way and Richard T. Jameson in *Movietone News*, no. 51 (August 1976), pp. 28–29.

Bernstein, Judith. "The Valley of the Shadow." *Focus!*, no. 8 (Autumn 1972), pp. 13–17. An interesting discussion of the *Rio Bravo/El Dorado/Rio Lobo* trilogy.

Bogdanovich, Peter. *The Cinema of Howard Hawks*. New York: Museum of Modern Art, 1962. The historical importance of this first attempt to evaluate the whole of the Hawksian cinema is evidenced by the fact that it was twice reprinted, in *Movie*, no. 5 (December 1962), pp. 8–18, and in *Cahiers du Cinéma*, no. 139 (January 1963), pp. 5–56.

————. "Hatari!" *Film Culture*, no. 25 (Summer 1962), pp. 24–25. "Anyone who does not see the beauty and brilliance of this picture is either a fool or a snob."

————. "El Dorado." In *Focus on Howard Hawks*. Edited by Joseph McBride. Englewood Cliffs: Prentice-Hall, 1972, pp. 147–50. Written a decade after his Hawks monograph, this discussion by Bogdanovich of *El Dorado* continues to present Hawks in terms of professionalism and a tragic world view.

Byron, Stuart. "*Auteurism*, Hawks, *Hatari!* and Me." In *Favorite Movies*. Edited by Philip Nobile. New York: Macmillan, 1973, pp. 254–67. "It is my proposal that Hawks should be understood as a Darwinian without regrets," writes Byron in arguing that *Hatari!* is "Hawks's greatest film."

Cavell, Stanley. "Leopards in Connecticut." *The Georgia Review* 30, no. 2 (Summer 1976):233–62. Cavell's essay on *Bringing Up Baby* is essential reading and goes a long way toward refuting the standard view of the comedies [an "alternate" version of the essay, shorter but also quite different, was published in *Quarterly Review of Film Studies* 2, no. 2 (May 1977):141–58 as part of the proceedings of the 1975 CUNY-NEH Conference on Film and the University].

Corliss, Richard. *Talking Pictures*. Woodstock, N.Y.: The Overlook Press, 1974. Corliss recasts the standard view of Hawks in terms of his screenwriting collaborators. Of special interest are Corliss's discussions of *Ball of Fire, Red River*, and *Gentlemen Prefer Blondes*.

————, ed. *The Hollywood Screenwriters*. New York: Avon Books, 1962. Four sections are of special interest: Corliss's introduction and his discussion of Ben Hecht, Richard Koszarski's discussion of Jules Furthman, and an interview with Bordon Chase by Jim Kitses.

Durgnat, Raymond. "Hawks Isn't Good Enough." *Film Comment* 13, no. 4 (July–August 1977):8–19. Durgnat's quirky attempt to debunk Hawks and his auteurist partisans (see William Paul's reply—listed below).

————. "Durgnat vs. Paul." *Film Comment* 14, no. 2 (March–April 1978):64–68. The "last round in the great Hawks debate."

Farber, Manny. *Negative Space*. New York: Praeger, 1971. The first two chapters, "Underground Films" (*Commentary*, November 1957) and "Howard Hawks" (*Artforum*, April 1969), are often cited as seminal pieces of Hawks scholarship. The latter essay is especially good on *Scarface* and *Red River*.

Ford, Greg. "Mostly on Rio Lobo." In *Focus on Howard Hawks*. Edited by Joseph McBride. Englewood Cliffs, N.J.: Prentice-Hall, 1972, pp. 150–62. Especially interesting for its discussion of the use of space in the Western trilogy.

Gili, Jean A. *Howard Hawks*. Paris: Editions Seghers, 1971. For those who read French, Gili's book is an essential text. His comments on sexual relations in Hawks and on the silent films are particularly interesting.

Gregory, Charles. "Knight Without Meaning?" *Sight and Sound* 42, no. 3 (Summer 1973):155–59. An insightful discussion of Hollywood's treatment of Chandler's Philip Marlowe character with special attention devoted to *The Big Sleep*.

Haskell, Molly. "The Cinema of Howard Hawks." *Intellectual Digest*, April 1972, pp. 56–58. The interest in all of Haskell's work on Hawks revolves around her description of sexual relationships in the films. In many respects this essay is the clearest and most useful explication of her position.

————. "*Man's Favorite Sport?* (Revisited)." In *Focus on Howard Hawks*. Edited by Joseph McBride. Englewood Cliffs, N.J.: Prentice-Hall, 1972, pp. 135–38. A cogent defense of an undervalued film.

————. *From Reverence to Rape*. New York: Holt, Rinehart and Winston, 1973, 1974. Haskell's chapters on "The Thirties" and "The Forties" are particularly good on *His Girl Friday* and *To Have and Have Not*.

————. "Howard Hawks: Masculine Feminine." *Film Comment* 10, no. 2 (March–April 1974):34–40. Very Wollenesque in certain respects, this version of the Haskell thesis is most interesting for her remarks on *Gentlemen Prefer Blondes*.

Henderson, Brian. "Romantic Comedy Today: Semi-Tough or Impossible." *Film Quarterly* 31, no. 4 (Summer 1978):11–23. This essay on the genre of romantic comedy is centrally concerned with *Semi-Tough*, both as comic novel and comic film. In passing, however, Henderson makes some interesting observations on *Bringing Up Baby, His Girl Friday*, and on Hawks's films generally.

Jameson, Richard T. "Talking and Doing in Rio Bravo." *Velvet Light Trap*, no. 12 (Spring 1974), pp. 26–31. A marvelous discussion of language as a mode of action in *Rio Bravo*.

———. "People Who Need People." *Movietone News*, no. 40 (April 1975), pp. 11–14. *To Have and Have Not* "is firstly and most durably a movie about the making of this particular movie."

Kawin, Bruce. *Faulkner and Film*. New York: Frederick Ungar Publishing Co., 1977. Kawin's long fourth chapter, "Turnabout: Faulkner's Films," includes extended discussions of *Today We Live, The Road to Glory, The Big Sleep*, and *Land of the Pharaohs*.

———. *To Have and Have Not*. Madison: University of Wisconsin Press, 1980. Kawin's introduction to the Furthman/Faulkner screenplay is easily the most sustained discussion of Hawks's working methods and his relationships with collaborators.

Leach, Jim. "The Screwball Comedy." In *Film Genre: Theory and Criticism*. Edited by Barry K. Grant. Metuchen, N.J.: The Scarecrow Press, 1977, pp. 75–89. Leach has much to say on Hawks in this overview of the screwball genre.

Luhr, William. "Howard Hawks: Hawksthief." *Wide Angle* 1, no. 2 (Summer 1976):10–20. Clearly the best of the many articles which take the similarity of *Rio Bravo, El Dorado*, and *Rio Lobo* as their point of departure. Luhr's essay also provides an interesting overview discussion of the Hawksian style.

McBride, Joseph, ed. *Focus on Howard Hawks*. Englewood Cliffs, N.J.: Prentice-Hall, 1972. An intelligently selected anthology of articles on Hawks. (Articles are entered separately by author.)

McNiven, Roger. "Howard Hawks' 'Monkey Business.'" *Bright Lights* 1, no. 3 (Spring 1975):23–26. McNiven discusses "Hawks' behavioral method" in *Monkey Business*, relative both to style (scientific, observational) and to character.

Monaco, James. "Notes on 'The Big Sleep'/Thirty Years After." *Sight and Sound* 44, no. 1 (Winter 1974/1975):34–39. *The Big Sleep*, writes Monaco, "is a summary of [Hawks's] world which depends equally on the wit and tone of the earlier comedies and the harsh existential mood of the gangster films."

Murphy, Kathleen. "Howard Hawks: An American Auteur in the Hemingway Tradition." Ph.D. dissertation, University of Washington, 1977. This is clearly the most thorough study of Hawks to date. The Hawks/Hemingway comparison forces Murphy to overemphasize the standard

"Hawks as existentialist" viewpoint, but it is difficult to imagine a more thoughtful and sophisticated explication of that position. Especially interesting are her discussions of Hawks's early sound films and of the role of women in Hawks, particularly in Hawksian comedy.

————. "Of Babies, Bones and Butterflies." *Movietone News*, No. 54 (June 1977), pp. 14–25. This marvelous essay on *Bringing Up Baby* is excerpted from Murphy's dissertation.

Paul, William. "Hawks vs. Durgnat." *Film Comment* 14, no. 1 (January–February 1978):68–71. Paul's eloquent defense of Hawks is far more interesting than Durgnat's original attack; Durgnat is to be thanked for provoking Paul's reply. Especially interesting are Paul's remarks on *Only Angels Have Wings* and *Rio Bravo*.

Peary, Gerald, and Groark, Stephen. "Hawks at Warner Brothers: 1932." *Velvet Light Trap*, no. 1 (June 1971), pp. 12–17. Useful discussions of *The Crowd Roars* and *Tiger Shark* (Peary's section on *The Crowd Roars* is reprinted in McBride).

Perkins, V. F. "Comedies." *Movie*, No. 5 (December 1962), pp. 21–22. Reprinted in *Movie Reader*. Edited by Ian Cameron. New York: Praeger, 1972, pp. 57–58. Perkins discusses the "ruthlessness" and "excess" of films like *Bringing Up Baby* and *Monkey Business*, but he concludes that Hawks's "comedies do not lament human degradation so much as celebrate human resilience."

————. "Hatari!" *Movie*, no. 5 (December 1962), pp. 28–30. Reprinted in *Movie Reader*. Edited by Ian Cameron. New York: Praeger, 1972, pp. 61–63. A fine essay in several respects, its primary interest now resides in its discussion of the attitude embodied in the Hawksian style.

Rivette, Jacques. "Génie de Howard Hawks." *Cahiers du Cinéma*, No. 23 (May 1953). Reprinted as "Rivette on Hawks," *Movie*, No. 5 (December 1962) and as "The Genius of Howard Hawks." In *Focus on Howard Hawks*. Edited by Joseph McBride. Englewood Cliffs, N.J.: Prentice-Hall, 1972, pp. 70–77. Though it focuses primarily on *Monkey Business*, Rivette's essay did much to set the terms for subsequent debate on all aspects of the Hawksian vision and style.

Rothman, William. "To Have and Have Not Adapted a Novel." In *The Modern American Novel and the Movies*. Edited by Gerald Peary and Roger Shatzkin. New York: Frederick Ungar Publishing Co., 1978, pp. 70–79. Rothman argues convincingly that "the affinity between Hawks and Hemingway must not be overemphasized. For Hemingway, . . . man is ultimately alone—tragically and nobly alone. For Hawks, man is by nature social. Although human society can all too readily be poisoned by those (e.g., Fascists) who are ultimately unwilling or unable to acknowledge their humanity, Hawks continually celebrates the positive values of true human community. . . . Hawks believes, specifically, in sexuality, in spontaneous music making, in wit, and in making films which both celebrate and exemplify such positivities."

Sarris, Andrew. "The World of Howard Hawks." In *Focus on Howard
    Hawks*. Edited by Joseph McBride. Englewood Cliffs, N.J.: Prentice-
    Hall, 1972, pp. 35–64. An early example of the Hawks-as-bitter-stoic
    argument; originally published in two parts in *Films and Filming* 8, no.
    10 (July 1962):20–23+, and no. 11 (August 1962):44–48.
———. "Howard Hawks." In *The American Cinema*. New York: E. P.
    Dutton, 1968. A capsule and very influential version of the argument
    that the Hawksian world view is "distinctively bitter."
———. Review of *El Dorado*. In *Confessions of a Cultist*. New York: Simon
    and Schuster, 1971, pp. 299–302. This *Village Voice* review is consistent
    with Sarris's earlier work in describing "humor and affirmation on the
    brink of despair" as the "poetic ingredients of the Hawksian western."
Shatzkin, Roger. "Who Cares Who Killed Owen Taylor?" In *The Modern
    American Novel and the Movies*. Edited by Gerald Peary and Roger
    Shatzkin. New York: Frederick Ungar Publishing Co., 1978, pp. 80–94.
    Clearly the best of the many articles comparing Chandler's novel with
    the Hawks film: "Chandler's story of his hero's failed individualistic and
    Romantic quest becomes on screen a dark romantic comedy that
    explores the feasibility of human sexual commitment between a man and
    a woman."
Shivas, Mark. "Blondes." *Movie*, no. 5 (December 1962), pp. 23–24. Re-
    printed in *Movie Reader*. Edited by Ian Cameron. New York: Praeger,
    1972, pp. 59–60. An early instance of the argument that "it's the girls
    who wear the trousers in the world of Howard Hawks."
Thompson, Richard. "Hawks at Seventy." In *Focus on Howard Hawks*.
    Edited by Joseph McBride. Englewood Cliffs, N.J.: Prentice-Hall,
    1972, pp. 139–46. A largely convincing defense of the underrated *Red
    Line 7000*.
Thomson, David. "All Along the River." *Sight and Sound* 46, no. 1 (Winter
    1976/1977):9–13. A major critic "revisits" the "glorious illusion" of *Red
    River*.
Wexman, Virginia Wright. "Kinesics and Film Acting: Humphrey Bogart in
    The Maltese Falcon and *The Big Sleep*." *Journal of Popular Film* 7, no. 1
    (1978):42–55. Wexman's remarks on gesture-play and body-language in
    The Big Sleep are especially insightful.
Willis, Donald C. *The Films of Howard Hawks*. Metuchen, N.J.: The Scare-
    crow Press, 1975. Willis seems torn between a love for Hawks's films and
    an extreme dislike of most Hawks criticism—for taking Hawks too
    seriously.
Wise, Naomi. "The Hawksian Woman." *Take One* 3, no. 3 (April 1972):17–19.
    One of the earliest and best of the articles praising Hawks for his positive
    treatment of women.
Wollen, Peter. *Signs and Meaning in the Cinema*. Revised edition.
    Bloomington: Indiana University Press, 1972. The first edition, pub-
    lished in 1969, was especially influential for its discussion of the auteur
    theory and Howard Hawks.

Wood, Robin. "Rio Bravo." *Movie*, no. 5 (December 1962), pp. 25–27. Much of Wood's "Cinema World" book on Hawks—including most of his discussion of *Rio Bravo*—appeared first as a two-part article, "Who the Hell is Howard Hawks?" *Focus!*, no. 1 (February 1967), pp. 3–6, and no. 2 (March 1967), pp. 8–18. The *Movie* essay on *Rio Bravo*, while clearly related to the *Rio Bravo* chapter in the book, is *very* different in its tone (strongly anti-Ford) and in many of its details.

———. *Howard Hawks*. London: Secker & Warburg; Garden City, N.Y.: Doubleday, 1968. The second of Wood's many fine books on major film directors.

———. "To Have (Written) and Have Not (Directed)." *Film Comment* 9, no. 3 (May–June 1973):30–35. Wood discusses the complexities of film authorship and concludes that *To Have and Have Not* is both "totally Hollywood and totally Hawks."

———. "Acting Up." *Film Comment* 12, no. 2 (March–April 1976):20–25. Wood discusses the opening scene of *The Big Sleep* in the context of an argument regarding the critical status of film acting.

———. *Personal Views*. London: Gordon Fraser, 1976. Two chapters are of especial interest to Hawks studies: "Reflections on the Auteur Theory" and "Hawks De-Wollenized."

———. "Responsibilities of a Gay Film Critic." *Film Comment* 14, no. 1 (January–February 1978):12–17. Wood discusses the way in which his view of Hawks "has changed and widened somewhat" since the publication of his Hawks book. Whether Wood's view has changed—or has become "wider" in the process—is not, in my view, as self-evident as Wood wants to believe.

Filmography

Silent Films

THE ROAD TO GLORY (Fox, 1926)
Producer: William Fox
Assistant Director: James Tinling
Screenplay: L. G. Rigby, from a story by Hawks
Cinematographer: Joseph August
Cast: May McAvoy (Judith Allen), Leslie Fenton (David Hale), Ford Sterling (James Allen), Rockliffe Fellows (Del Cole)
Running Time: 70 minutes
Premier: February 7, 1926
(Note: This apparently lost film has no relationship to Hawks's later *The Road to Glory*, adapted from Roland Dorgeles's film in 1936.)

FIG LEAVES (Fox, 1926)
Producer: Howard Hawks
Supervision: Winfield R. Sheehan
Assistant Director: James Tinling
Screenplay: Hope Loring, Louis D. Lighton, from a story by Hawks
Titles: Malcolm Stuart Boylan
Cinematographer: Joseph August (two sequences in Technicolor)
Art Directors: William S. Darling, William Cameron Menzies
Costumes: Adrian
Editor: Rose Smith
Cast: George O'Brien (Adam Smith), Olive Borden (Eve Smith), Phyllis Haver (Alice Atkins), Andre de Beranger (Joseph Andre), William Austin (Andre's Assistant), Heinie Conklin (Eddie McSwiggen)
Running Time: 72 minutes
Premier: August 22, 1926
16 mm. Rental: Films Inc.

THE CRADLE SNATCHERS (Fox, 1927)
Producer: Howard Hawks
Assistant Director: James Tinling
Screenplay: Sarah Y. Mason, from the play by Russell Medcraft and Norma Mitchell
Titles: Malcolm Stuart Boylan
Setting: William Darling
Costumes: Kathleen Kay
Cinematographer: L. William O'Connell
Editor: Ralph Dixon
Cast: Louise Fazenda (Susan Martin), J. Farrell MacDonald (George Martin), Ethel Wales (Ethel Drake), Franklin Pangborn (Howard Drake), Dorothy Phillips (Kitty Ladd), William Davidson (Roy Ladd), Joseph Striker (Joe Valley), Nick Stuart (Henry Winton), Arthur Lake (Oscar), Sally Eilers, Diane Ellis
Running Time: 70 minutes
Premier: May 28, 1927 (New York); released June 5

PAID TO LOVE (Fox, 1927)
Producer: Howard Hawks
Assistant Director: James Tinling
Screenplay: William M. Conselman, Seton I. Miller, from a story by Harry Carr
Adaptation: Benjamin Glazer
Titles: Malcolm Stuart Boylan
Cinematographer: L. William O'Connell
Art Director: William S. Darling
Editor: Ralph Dixon
Cast: George O'Brien (Crown Prince Michael), Virginia Valli (Dolores/ Gaby), J. Farrell MacDonald (Peter Roberts), Thomas Jefferson (King), William Powell (Prince Eric)
Running Time: 80 minutes
Premier: July 23, 1927 (New York); released August 14

A GIRL IN EVERY PORT (Fox, 1928)
Producer: Howard Hawks
Assistant Director: William Tummel
Screenplay: Seton I. Miller, Reginald Morris, Sidney Lanford, from a story by Hawks and a screenstory by James K. McGuiness
Titles: Malcolm Stuart Boylan
Cinematographers: L. William O'Connell, R. J. Berguist
Art Directors: William S. Darling, Leo E. Kuter
Costumes: Kathleen Kay

Editor: Ralph Dixon
Cast: Victor McLaglen (Spike Madden), Robert Armstrong (Bill), Louise Brooks (Tessie), Leila Hyams, Sally Rand, Myrna Loy, William Demarest
Running time: 64 minutes
Premier: February 26, 1928
16 mm. Rental: The Killiam Collection

FAZIL (Fox, 1928)
Producer: William Fox
Assistant Director: James Tinling
Screenplay: Seton I. Miller, Philip Klein, from the play *L'Insoumise*, by Pierre Frondaie, and the English adaptation, *Prince Fazil*
Cinematographer: L. William O'Connell
Editor: Ralph Dixon
Cast: Charles Farrell (Prince Fazil), Greta Nissen (Fabienne), Mae Busch (Helene Debreuze), John Boles (John Clavering), Tyler Brooke (Jacques Debreuze), Vadim Uraneff (Ahmed)
Running Time: 95 minutes
Premier: June 4, 1928, released in both sound effects plus musical score and silent versions

THE AIR CIRCUS (Fox, 1928) (part talking)
Producer: William Fox
Assistant Director: William Tummel
Codirector: Lewis Seiler (talking sequences)
Dialogue Director: Charles Judels
Screenplay: Seton I. Miller, Norman Z. McLeod, from a story by Graham Baker and Andrew Bennison
Dialogue: Hugh Herbert
Titles: William Kernell
Cinematographer: Dan Clark
Editor: Ralph Dixon
Cast: Louise Dresser (Mrs. Blake), David Rollins (Buddy Blake), Arthur Lake (Speed Doolittle), Sue Carol (Sue Manning), Charles Delany (Charles Manning), Heinie Conklin (Jerry McSwiggen), Earl Robinson (Lt. Blake)
Running Time: 100 minutes
Premier: September 30, 1928

TRENT'S LAST CASE (Fox, 1929)
Producer: Howard Hawks
Supervision: Bertram Millhauser
Assistant Director: E. D. Leshin

Screenplay: Scott Darling, Beulah Marie Dix, from E. C. Bentley's novel
Titles: Malcolm Stuart Boylan
Cinematographer: Hal Rosson
Costumes: Sophie Wachner
Cast: Donald Crisp (Sigsbee Manderson), Raymond Griffith (Philip Trent), Raymond Hatton (Joshua Cupples), Marceline Day (Evelyn Manderson), Lawrence Gray (Jack Marlowe), Anita Garvin, Edgar Kennedy (Police Inspector)
Running Time: 67 minutes
Premier: March 31, 1929, released in both sound effects plus musical score and silent versions

Talking Pictures

THE DAWN PATROL (First National–Warner Brothers, 1930)
Producer: Robert North
Screenplay: Howard Hawks, Dan Totheroh, Seton I. Miller, from a story written by Hawks but credited to John Monk Saunders
Cinematographer: Ernest Haller
Aerial Sequences: Leo Nomis
Assistant Director: Elmer Dyer
Art Director: Jack Okey
Music: Leo F. Forbstein
Editor: Ray Curtiss
Special Effects: Fred Jackman
Cast: Richard Barthelmess (Dick Courtney), Douglas Fairbanks, Jr. (Douglas Scott), Neil Hamilton (Major Brand), William Janney (Gordon Scott), James Finlayson (Field Sergeant), Frank McHugh (Flaherty), Gardner James (Ralph Hollister)
Running Time: 95 minutes
Premier: July 10, 1930 (New York); released August 20
16 mm. Rental: United Artists/16

THE CRIMINAL CODE (Columbia, 1931)
Producers: Howard Hawks, Harry Cohn
Screenplay: Seton I. Miller, Fred Niblo, Jr., from the play by Martin Flavin
Cinematographers: James Wong Howe, L. William O'Connell
Art Director: Edward Jewell
Sound: Glen Rominger
Editor: Edward Curtis
Cast: Walter Huston (Warden Brady), Phillips Holmes (Robert Graham), Constance Cummings (Mary Brady), DeWitt Jennings (Gleason), John Sheehan (MacManus), Boris Karloff (Galloway), Clark Marshall (Runch), Andy Devine
Running Time: 97 minutes

Premier: January 15, 1931
16 mm. Rental: Audio Brandon Films

SCARFACE (Atlantic Pictures/United Artists, 1932)
Producers: Howard Hawks, Howard Hughes
Assistant Director: Richard Rosson
Screenplay: Ben Hecht, Seton I. Miller, John Lee Mahin, W. R. Burnett,
from the novel by Armitage Trail
Cinematographers: Lee Garmes, L. William O'Connell
Art Director: Harry Oliver
Production Manager: Charles Stallings
Music: Adolph Tandler, Gus Arnheim
Sound: William Snyder
Editors: Edward Curtis, Douglas Biggs
Cast: Paul Muni (Tony Camonte), Ann Dvorak (Cesca), Karen Morley
(Poppy), George Raft (Guino Rinaldo), Osgood Perkins (Johnny Lovo), Boris
Karloff (Gaffney), Vinie Barnett (Angelo), C. Henry Gordon (Guarino), Inez
Palange (Mrs. Camonte), Edwin Maxwell (Chief of Detectives)
Running Time: 90 minutes
Premier: April 9, 1932
16 mm. Rental: Swank

THE CROWD ROARS (Warner Brothers, 1932)
Screenplay: Kubec Glasmon, John Bright, Seton I. Miller, Niven Busch,
from a story by Hawks
Cinematographer: Sid Hickox
Art Director: Jack Okey
Music: Leo F. Forbstein
Editors: John Stumar, Thomas Pratt
Technical Effects: Fred Jackman
Cast: James Cagney (Joe Greer), Joan Blondell (Anne), Ann Dvorak (Lee),
Eric Linden (Eddie Greer), Guy Kibbee (Dad Greer), Frank McHugh
(Spud), Charlotte Merriam (Mrs. Spud Smith), Harry Hartz, Fred Frame
(drivers)
Running Time: 85 minutes
Premier: April 16, 1932
16 mm. Rental: United Artists/16

TIGER SHARK (First National/Warner Brothers, 1932)
Assistant Director: Richard Rosson
Marine Supervision: Guy Silva
Screenplay: Wells Root, from the story "Tuna" by Houston Branch
Cinematographer: Tony Gaudio

Art Director: Jack Okey
Music: Leo F. Forbstein
Costumes: Orry-Kelly
Editor: Thomas Pratt
Cast: Edward G. Robinson (Mike Mascarenhas), Richard Arlen (Pipes Boley), Zita Johann (Quita Silva), Vince Barnett (Fishbone), J. Carrol Nash (Tony), William Ricciardi (Manuel Silva)
Running Time: 80 minutes
Premier: September 24, 1932
16 mm. Rental: United Artists/16

TODAY WE LIVE (MGM, 1933)
Producer: Howard Hawks
Screenplay: Edith Fitzgerald, Dwight Taylor, William Faulkner, from the story "Turnabout," by Faulkner
Cinematographer: Oliver T. Marsh
Editor: Edward Curtis
Cast: Joan Crawford (Diana), Gary Cooper (Bogard), Robert Young (Claude), Franchot Tone (Ronnie), Roscoe Karns (McGinnis)
Running Time: 113 minutes
Premier: March 3, 1933
16 mm. Rental: Films Inc.

VIVA VILLA! (MGM, 1934)
Producer: David O. Selznick
Directors: Jack Conway (and, uncredited, Howard Hawks)
Assistant Director: James D. Waters
Screenplay: Ben Hecht, Hawks (uncredited), from the story by Edgcumb Pinchon and O. B. Stade
Cinematographers: James Wong Howe, Charles G. Clarke
Art Director: Harry Oliver
Sets: Edwin B. Willis
Music: Herbert Stothart, Juan Aguilar
Editor: Robert J. Kern
Cast: Wallace Beery (Pancho Villa), Leo Carrillo (Sierra), Fay Wray (Teresa), Stuart Erwin (Johnny Sykes), Donald Cook (Don Felipe), Henry B. Walthall (Madero), Joseph Schildkraut (General Pascal)
Running Time: 115 minutes
Premier: April 27, 1934
16 mm Rental: Films Inc.

TWENTIETH CENTURY (Columbia, 1934)
Producer: Howard Hawks
Screenplay: Ben Hecht, Charles MacArthur, from their play, based on the Charles Bruce Milholland play *Napoleon on Broadway*
Cinematographers: Joseph August, Joseph Walker
Editor: Gene Havlick
Cast: John Barrymore (Oscar Jaffe), Carole Lombard (Lily Garland), Walter Connolly (Oliver Webb), Roscoe Karns (Owen O'Malley), Charles Levison (Max Jacobs), Edgar Kennedy (McGonigle), Etienne Girardot (Matthew Clark)
Running Time: 91 minutes
Premier: May 11, 1934
16 mm Rental: Swank, Audio Brandon Films

BARBARY COAST (Goldwyn Productions/United Artists, 1935)
Producer: Samuel Goldwyn
Assistant Director: Walter Mayo
Screenplay: Ben Hecht, Charles MacArthur (and Edward Chodorov)
Cinematographer: Ray June
Art Director: Richard Day
Music: Alfred Newman
Costumes: Omar Kiam
Cast: Miriam Hopkins (Mary), Edward G. Robinson (Louis Chamalis), Joel McCrea (James Carmichael), Walter Brennan (Old Atrocity), Frank Craven (Col. Cobb), Brian Donlevy (Knuckles), Harry Carey (Slocum), Donald Meek (Sawbuck McTavish)
Running Time: 91 minutes
Premier: September 27, 1935
16 mm. Rental: Audio Brandon Films

CEILING ZERO (Cosmopolitan/First National–Warner Brothers, 1936)
Producer: Harry Joe Brown
Screenplay: Frank Wead, from his play
Cinematographer: Arthur Edeson
Art Director: John Hughes
Music: Leo F. Forbstein
Editor: William Holmes
Special Effects: Fred Jackman
Technical Advisor: Paul Mantz
Cast: James Cagney (Dizzy Davis), Pat O'Brien (Jake Lee), June Travis

(Tommy), Stuart Erwin (Texas Clarke), Isabel Jewell (Lou Clarke), Henry Wadsworth (Tay)
Running Time: 95 minutes
Premier: January 25, 1936

THE ROAD TO GLORY (Twentieth Century–Fox, 1936)
Producer: Darryl F. Zanuck
Associate Producer: Nunnally Johnson
Assistant Director: Ed O'Fearna
Screenplay: Joel Sayre, William Faulkner, from the film *Les Croix de Bois*, by Roland Dorgeles
Cinematographer: Gregg Toland
Art Director: Hans Peters
Sets: Thomas Little
Music: Louis Silvers
Costumes: Gwen Wakeling
Editor: Edward Curtis
Cast: Fredric March (Lt. Michel Denet), Warner Baxter (Capt. Paul Laroche), Lionel Barrymore (Papa Laroche), June Lang (Monique), Gregory Ratoff (Bouffiou), Victor Kilian (Regnier)
Running Time: 95 minutes
Premier: June 2, 1936
16 mm. Rental: Films Inc.

COME AND GET IT (Goldwyn Productions/United Artists, 1936)
Producer: Samuel Goldwyn
Directors: Howard Hawks, William Wyler (disclaimed)
Assistant Directors: Richard Rosson, Ross Lederman
Screenplay: Jane Murfin, Jules Furthman, from the novel by Edna Ferber
Cinematographers: Gregg Toland, Rudolph Mate
Art Director: Richard Day
Sets: Julia Heron
Music: Alfred Newman
Costumes: Omar Kiam
Editor: Edward Curtis
Special Effects: Ray Binger
Cast: Edward Arnold (Barney Glasgow), Frances Farmer (Lotta), Joel McCrea (Richard Glasgow), Walter Brennan (Swan Bostrom), Frank Shields (Tony Schwerke), Andrea Leeds (Evvie Glasgow), Mary Nash (Emma Louise Glasgow)
Running Time: 105 minutes
Premier: October 29, 1936
16 mm. Rental: Audio Brandon Films

BRINGING UP BABY (RKO, 1938)
Producer: Howard Hawks
Associate Producer: Cliff Reid
Assistant Director: Edward Donahue
Screenplay: Dudley Nichols, Hagar Wilde (and, uncredited, Robert McGowan and Gertrude Purcell?), from a story by Wilde
Cinematographer: Russell Metty
Art Directors: Van Nest Polglase, Perry Ferguson
Sets: Darrell Silvera
Music: Roy Webb
Editor: George Hively
Special Effects: Vernon L. Walker
Cast: Cary Grant (David Huxley), Katharine Hepburn (Susan Vance), Charles Ruggles (Major Horace Applegate), Walter Catlett (Slocum), Barry Fitzgerald (Gogarty), May Robson (Aunt Elizabeth), Fritz Feld (Dr. Lehmann), Virginia Walker (Alice Swallow), George Irving (Peabody), Leona Roberts (Mrs. Gogarty), Tala Birell (Mrs. Lehmann)
Running Time: 102 minutes
Premier: February 18, 1938
16 mm. Rental: Films Inc.

ONLY ANGELS HAVE WINGS (Columbia, 1939)
Producer: Howard Hawks
Assistant Director: Arthur Black
Screenplay: Jules Furthman (and, uncredited, William Rankin and Eleanore Griffin?), from a story by Hawks
Cinematographers: Joseph Walker, Elmer Dyer
Art Director: Lionel Banks
Music: Dimitri Tiomkin
Gowns: Kalloch
Editor: Viola Lawrence
Special Effects: E. Roy Davidson, Edwin C. Hahn
Technical Advisor and Chief Pilot: Paul Mantz
Cast: Cary Grant (Jeff Carter), Jean Arthur (Bonnie Lee), Thomas Mitchell (Kid Dabb), Richard Barthelmess (Bat McPherson), Sig Ruman (Dutchy), Rita Hayworth (Judith), Victor Kilian (Sparks), John Carrol (Gent Shelton), Allyn Joslyn (Les Peters), Noah Beery, Jr. (Joe Souther), Melissa Sierra (Lily)
Running Time: 121 minutes
Premier: May 25, 1939
16 mm. Rental: Audio Brandon Films

HIS GIRL FRIDAY (Columbia, 1940)
Producer: Howard Hawks
Assistant Director: Clifton Broughton

Screenplay: Charles Lederer, from the play *The Front Page*, by Ben Hecht and Charles MacArthur
Cinematographer: Joseph Walker
Art Director: Lionel Banks
Music: Morris Stoloff
Gowns: Kalloch
Editor: Gene Havlick
Cast: Cary Grant (Walter Burns), Rosalind Russell (Hildy Johnson), Ralph Bellamy (Bruce Baldwin), Gene Lockhart (Sheriff Hartwell), Abner Biberman (Diamond Louie), Porter Hall (Murphy), Ernest Truex (Bensinger), Clarence Kolb (Mayor), Roscoe Karns (McCue), Frank Orth (Duffy), John Qualen (Earl Williams), Helen Mack (Mollie Malloy), Alma Kruger (Mrs. Baldwin), Billy Gilbert (Joe Pettibone), Edwin Maxwell (Dr. Egelhoffer)
Running Time: 92 minutes
Premier: January 18, 1940
16 mm. Rental: Audio Brandon Films, Universal 16

SERGEANT YORK (Warner Brothers, 1941)
Producers: Jesse L. Lasky, Hal B. Wallis
Screenplay: Abem Finkel, Harry Chandler, Howard Koch, John Huston, from *War Diary of Sergeant York*, edited by Tom Skeyhill, and *Sergeant York–Last of the Long Hunters*, by Skeyhill
Cinematographers: Sol Polito, Arthur Edeson (war sequence)
Art Director: John Hughes
Sets: Fred MacLean
Music: Max Steiner
Musical Director: Leo F. Forbstein
Sound: Nathan Levinson
Makeup: Perc Westmore
Editor: William Holmes
Cast: Gary Cooper (Alvin C. York), Walter Brennan (Pastor Rosier Pile), Joan Leslie (Gracie Williams), George Tobias (Pusher Rose), Stanley Ridges (Major Buxton), Margaret Wycherley (Mother York), Ward Bond (Ike Botkin), Noah Beery, Jr. (Buck Lipscomb), June Lockhart (Rosie York), Dickie Moore (George York)
Running Time: 134 minutes
Premier: September 9, 1941
16 mm. Rental: United Artists/16

BALL OF FIRE (RKO, 1941)
Producer: Samuel Goldwyn
Assistant Director: William Tummel
Screenplay: Billy Wilder, Charles Brackett, from the story "From A to Z," by Wilder and Thomas Monroe
Cinematographer: Gregg Toland

Art Director: Perry Ferguson
Assistant: McClure Claps
Sets: Howard Bristol
Music: Alfred Newman
Costumes: Edith Head
Editor: Daniel Mandell
Cast: Gary Cooper (Bertram Potts), Barbara Stanwyck (Sugarpuss O'Shea), Richard Haydn (Professor Oddly), Oscar Homolka (Professor Gurkakoff), Dana Andrews (Joe Lilac), Dan Duryea (Duke Pastrami), Henry Travers (Professor Jerome), S.Z. Sakall (Professor Magenbruch), Tully Marshall (Professor Robinson), Leonid Kinskey (Professor Quintana), Aubrey Mather (Professor Peagram), Mary Field (Miss Totten), Kathleen Howard (Miss Brag)
Running Time: 111 minutes
Premier: January 9, 1942
16 mm Rental: Audio Brandon Films

AIR FORCE (Warner Brothers, 1943)
Producer: Hal B. Wallis
Assistant Director: Jack Sullivan
Screenplay: Dudley Nichols, William Faulkner (and, uncredited, Arthur Horman)
Cinematographer: James Wong Howe
Aerial Photography: Elmer Dyer, Charles Marshall
Art Director: John Hughes
Sets: Walter F. Tilford
Music: Franz Waxman
Musical Direction: Leo F. Forbstein
Editor: George Amy
Special Effects: E. Roy Davidson, Rex Wimpy, H. F. Koenekamp
Technical Advisor and Chief Pilot: Paul Mantz
Cast: John Garfield (Sgt. Winocki), John Ridgely (Capt. Quincannon), George Tobias (Corp. Weinberg), Harry Carey (Sgt. White), Gig Young (Lt. Williams), Arthur Kennedy (Lt. McMartin), Charles Drake (Lt. Hauser), James Brown (Lt. Tex Rader)
Running Time: 124 minutes
Premier: March 20, 1943
16 mm Rental: United Artists/16

TO HAVE AND HAVE NOT (Warner Brothers, 1944)
Producer: Howard Hawks
Assistant Director: Jack Sullivan
Screenplay: Jules Furthman, William Faulkner, from the novel by Ernest Hemingway
Cinematographer: Sidney Hickox

Art Director: Charles Novi
Sets: Casey Roberts
Music: Leo F. Forbstein. Original song, "How Little We Know," by Hoagy
Carmichael and Johnny Mercer
Editor: Christian Nyby
Special Effects: E. Roy Davidson, Rex Wimpy
Technical Advisor: Louis Comien
Gowns: Milo Anderson
Makeup: Perc Westmore
Cast: Humphrey Bogart (Harry Morgan), Walter Brennan (Eddie), Lauren
Bacall (Marie Brown/Slim), Hoagy Carmichael (Crickett), Marcel Dalio
(Frenchy Gerard), Walter Sande (Johnson), Dan Seymour (Capt. Reynard),
Walter Molnar (Paul de Bursac), Dolores Moran (Helène de Bursac), Shel-
don Leonard (Lt. Coyo), Aldo Nadi (bodyguard), Paul Marion (Beauclerc)
Running Time: 97 minutes
Premier: January 20, 1944
16 mm. Rental: United Artists/16

THE BIG SLEEP (Warner Brothers, 1946)
Producer: Howard Hawks
Assistant Director: Chuck Hansen
Screenplay: William Faulkner, Jules Furthman, Leigh Brackett, from the
novel by Raymond Chandler
Cinematographer: Sidney Hickox
Art Director: Carl Jules Weyl
Sets: Fred MacLean
Music: Max Steiner
Musical Director: Leo F. Forbstein
Wardrobe: Leah Rhodes
Editor: Christian Nyby
Special Effects: E. Roy Davidson, Warren E. Lynch
Cast: Humphrey Bogart (Philip Marlowe), Lauren Bacall (Vivian), John
Ridgely (Eddie Mars), Louis Jean Heydt (Joe Brody), Elisha Cook, Jr.
(Jones), Regis Toomey (Bernie Ohls), Sonia Darrin (Agnes), Bob Steele
(Canino), Martha Vickers (Carmen), Tom Rafferty (Carol Lundgren),
Dorothy Malone (girl in bookshop), Charles Waldren (General Sternwood),
Charles D. Brown (Norris), Tom Fadden (Sidney), Ben Welden (Pete),
Trevor Bardette (Art Huck), Joy Barlowe (cab driver), Peggy Knudsen (Mona
Mars), Theodore von Eltz (Geiger), Carole Douglas (librarian), Dan Wallace
(Owen Taylor)
Running Time: 114 minutes
Premier: August 31, 1946
16 mm. Rental: United Artists/16

RED RIVER (United Artists/Monterey, 1948)
Producer: Howard Hawks
Executive Producer: Charles K. Feldman
Assistant Director: William McGarry
Second Unit Director: Arthur Rosson
Screenplay: Bordon Chase, Charles Schnee, from the book *Blazing Guns on the Chisholm Trail*, by Chase
Cinematographer: Russell Harlan
Art Director: John Datu Arensma
Music: Dimitri Tiomkin
Makeup: Lee Greenway
Editor: Christian Nyby
Special Effects: Don Steward
Special Photographic Effects: Allan Thompson
Cast: John Wayne (Tom Dunson), Montgomery Clift (Matthew Garth), Walter Brennan (Groot), John Ireland (Cherry Valance), Joanne Dru (Tess Millay), Noah Beery, Jr. (Buster), Chief Yowlachie (Quo), Paul Fix (Teeler), Hank Worden (Sims), Harry Carey, Sr. (Melville), Harry Carey, Jr. (Dan Latimer), Ivan Parry (Bunk Kennelly), Coleen Gray (Fen), Mickey Kuhn (Matthew as a boy), Hal Taliaferro (Old Leather), Paul Fiero (Fernandez), Ray Hyke, William Self (wounded wrangler), Dan White (Larcdo), Shelley Winters
Running Time: 125 minutes
Premier: August 20, 1948
16 mm. Rental: United Artists/16

A SONG IS BORN (RKO, 1948)
Producer: Samuel Goldwyn
Assistant Director: Joseph Boyle
Screenplay: Harry Tugend, based on Hawks's film *Ball of Fire*
Cinematographer: Gregg Toland
Art Directors: George Jenkins, Perry Ferguson
Music: Emil Newman, Hugo Friedhofer
Songs: Don Raye, Gene DePaul
Makeup: Robert Stephanoff
Editor: Daniel Mandell
Special Photographic Effects: John P. Fulton
Cast: Danny Kaye (Prof. Robert Frisbee), Virginia Mayo (Honey Swanson), Benny Goodman (Prof. Magenbruch), Hugh Herbert (Prof. Twingle), Steve Cochran (Tony Crow), J. Edward Bromberg (Dr. Elfini), Felix Bressart (Prof. Gurkakoff), Ludwig Stossel (Prof. Traumer), O. Z. Whithead (Prof. Oddly), Esther Dale (Miss Brag), Mary Field (Miss Totten)
Running Time: 113 minutes
Premier: November 6, 1948
16 mm. Rental: Audio Brandon Films

I WAS A MALE WAR BRIDE (Fox, 1949)
(You Can't Sleep Here)
Producer: Sol C. Siegel
Assistant Director: Arthur Jacobson
Screenplay: Charles Lederer, Leonard Spigelglass, Hagar Wilde, from the
magazine story by Henri Rochard
Cinematographers: Norbert Brodine, O. H. Borrodaile
Art Directors: Lyle Wheeler, Albert Hogsett
Sets: Thomas Little, Walter M. Scott
Music: Cyril Mockridge
Musical Director: Lionel Newman
Makeup: Ben Nye
Editor: James B. Clark
Special Photographic Effects: Fred Sersen
Cast: Cary Grant (Henri Rochard), Ann Sheridan (Catherine Gates), William
Neff (Capt. Jack Rumsey), Eugene Gericke (Warrant Officer Tony Jowitt),
Marion Marshall (Kitty) and Randy Stuart (WACs), Kenneth Tobey (Red)
Running Time: 105 minutes
Premier: September 1949
16 mm. Rental: Films Inc.

THE THING (RKO/Winchester, 1951)
(The Thing From Another World)
Producer: Howard Hawks
Associate Producer: Edward Lasker
Directors: Christian Nyby (and, uncredited, Hawks?)
Assistant Directors: Arthur Siteman, Max Henry
Screenplay: Charles Lederer, Hawks (and, uncredited, Ben Hecht?), from
the story "Who Goes There?" by John W. Campbell, Jr. (aka Don Stuart)
Cinematographer: Russell Harlan
Art Directors: Albert S. D'Agostino, John Hughes
Sets: Darrell Silvera, William Stevens
Music: Dimitri Tiomkin
Sound: Phil Brigandi, Clem Portman
Makeup: Lee Greenway
Editor: Roland Cross
Special Effects: Donald Steward
Special Photographic Effects: Linwood Dunn
Special Photography: Lee Nelows
Cast: Kenneth Tobey (Capt. Patrick Hendry), Margaret Sheridan (Nikki
Nicholson), Douglas Spencer (Scotty), Dewey Martin (Bob), Robert
Cornthwaite (Prof. Carrington), James Young (Lt. Eddie Dykes), Robert
Nichols (Lt. MacPherson), John Dierkes (Dr. Chapman), James Arness (The

Thing), William Self (Barnes)
Running Time: 85 minutes
Premier: April 1951
16 mm. Rental: Films Inc.

THE BIG SKY (RKO/Winchester, 1952)
Producer: Howard Hawks
Associate Producer: Edward Lasker
Assistant Director: William McGarry
Second Unit Director: Arthur Rosson
Screenplay: Dudley Nichols, from the novel by A. B. Guthrie, Jr.
Cinematographer: Russell Harlan
Art Directors: Albert S. D'Agostino, Perry Ferguson
Sets: Darrell Silvera, William Stevens
Music: Dimitri Tiomkin
Costumes: Dorothy Jeakins
Makeup: Mel Burns, Don Cash
Editor: Christian Nyby
Special Effects: Donald Steward
Cast: Kirk Douglas (Jim Deakins), Dewey Martin (Boone Caudill), Arthur
Hunnicutt (Zeb Calloway), Elizabeth Threatt (Teal Eye), Hank Worden
(Poordevil), Jim Davis (Streak), Buddy Baer (Romaine), Steven Geray (Jour-
donnais), Henri Letondal (Labadie), Paul Frees (McMasters), Barbara
Hawks
Running Time: 120 minutes
Premier: August 1952
16 mm. Rental: Films Inc.

O. HENRY'S FULL HOUSE (Twentieth Century–Fox, 1952)
"The Ransom of Red Chief" Episode
Producer: André Hakim
Screenplay: Nunnally Johnson, from the short story by O. Henry
Cinematographer: Milton Krasner
Art Director: Chester Goce
Music: Alfred Newman
Editor: William B. Murphy
Narrator: John Steinbeck
Cast: Fred Allen (Sam), Oscar Levant (Bill), Lee Aaker (J.B.), Kathleen
Freeman (J.B.'s mother), Alfred Mizner (J.B.'s father), Robert Easton
Running Time: 25 minutes
Premier: September 1952
16 mm. Rental: Films Inc.

MONKEY BUSINESS (Twentieth Century–Fox, 1952)
Producer: Sol C. Siegel
Screenplay: Ben Hecht, I. A. L. Diamond, Charles Lederer, from a story by Harry Segall
Cinematographer: Milton Krasner
Art Directors: Lyle Wheeler, George Patrick
Sets: Thomas Little, Walter M. Scott
Music: Leigh Harline
Musical Director: Lionel Newman
Makeup: Ben Nye
Editor: William B. Murphy
Special Photographic Effects: Ray Kellogg
Cast: Cary Grant (Prof. Barnaby Fulton), Ginger Rogers (Edwina Fulton), Charles Coburn (Oliver Oxly), Marilyn Monroe (Lois Laurel), Hugh Marlowe (Hank Entwhistle), Robert Cornthwaite (Dr. Zoldeck), Esther Dale, George Winslow (deep-voiced boy), Harry Carey, Jr., Heinie Conklin
Running Time: 97 minutes
Premier: September 1952
16 mm. Rental: Films Inc.

GENTLEMEN PREFER BLONDES (Twentieth Century–Fox, 1953)
Producer: Sol C. Siegel
Assistant Director: Paul Helmick
Screenplay: Charles Lederer, from the play by Anita Loos and Joseph Fields
Cinematographer: Harry J. Wild
Art Directors: Lyle Wheeler, Joseph C. Wright
Sets: Claude Carpenter
Choreography: Jack Cole
Songs: Jule Styne, Leo Robin, Hoagy Carmichael, Harold Adamson
Musical Director: Lionel Newman
Costumes: Travilla
Makeup: Ben Nye
Editor: Hugh S. Fowler
Special Photographic Effects: Ray Kellogg
Cast: Marilyn Monroe (Lorelei), Jane Russell (Dorothy), Charles Coburn (Sir Francis Beekman), Elliott Reid (Malone), Tommy Noonan (Gus Esmond), George Winslow (Henry Spofford III), Marcel Dalio (magistrate), Harry Carey, Jr. (Winslow)
Running Time: 91 minutes
Premier: August 1953
16 mm. Rental: Films Inc.

LAND OF THE PHARAOHS (Warner Brothers/Continental Company, 1955)
Producer: Howard Hawks
Associate Producer: Arthur Siteman
Assistant Director: Paul Helmick
Second Unit Director: Noel Howard
Screenplay: William Faulkner, Harry Kurnitz, Harold Jack Bloom
Cinematographers: Lee Garmes (interiors), Russell Harlan (exteriors) (Cinema Scope)
Art Director: Alexandre Trauner
Music: Dimitri Tiomkin
Costumes: Mayo
Makeup: Emile Lavigne
Editors: Rudi Fehr, V. Sagovsky
Special Effects: Don Steward
Cast: Jack Hawkins (Cheops the Pharaoh), Joan Collins (Princess Nellifer), Dewey Martin (Senta), Alexis Minotis (Hamar), James Robertson Justice (Vashtar), Luisa Boni (Kyra), Sydney Chaplin (Treneh), Kerima (Queen Nahilla)
Running Time: 101 minutes
Premier: July 2, 1955
16 mm. Rental: Audio Brandon, Budget Films

RIO BRAVO (Warner Brothers/Armada, 1959)
Producer: Howard Hawks
Assistant Director: Paul Helmick
Screenplay: Jules Furthman, Leigh Brackett, from a short story by Barbara Hawks McCampbell (and, uncredited, Howard Hawks)
Cinematographer: Russell Harlan
Art Director: Leo K. Kuter
Sets: Ralph S. Hurst
Music: Dimitri Tiomkin
Songs: Tiomkin, Paul Francis Webster
Costumes: Marjorie Best
Editor: Folmar Blangsted
Cast: John Wayne (John T. Chance), Dean Martin (Dude), Walter Brennan (Stumpy), Angie Dickinson (Feathers), Ricky Nelson (Colorado), Ward Bond (Pat Wheeler), John Russell (Nathan Burdett), Pedro Gonzalez-Gonzalez (Carlos), Estelita Rodriguez (Consuela), Claude Akins (Joe Burdett), Harry Carey, Jr. (Harold), Bob Terhune (bartender)
Running Time: 140 minutes
Premier: April 4, 1959
16 mm. Rental: Swank

HATARI! (Paramount/Malabar, 1962)
Producer: Howard Hawks
Associate Producer and Second Unit Director: Paul Helmick
Assistant Directors: Tom Connors, Russ Saunders
Screenplay: Leigh Brackett
Story: Harry Kurnitz
Cinematographers: Russell Harlan, Joseph Brun
Art Directors: Hal Pereira, Carl Anderson
Sets: Sam Comer, Claude Carpenter
Music: Henry Mancini
Song: "Just for Tonight," by Johnny Mercer and Hoagy Carmichael
Editor: Stuart Gilmore
Special Effects: John P. Fulton
Special Mechanical Effects: Richard Parker
Technical Advisor: Willy deBeer
Cast: John Wayne (Sean Mercer), Elsa Martinelli (Dallas), Hardy Kruger (Kurt), Gérard Blain (Chips), Red Buttons (Pockets), Michèle Girardon (Brandy), Bruce Cabot (Indian), Valentin de Vargas (Luis)
Running Time: 155 minutes
Premier: December 31, 1961 (Detroit); released June 20, 1962
16 mm. Rental: Films Inc., Paramount Non-Theatrical

MAN'S FAVORITE SPORT? (Universal/Gibraltar/Laurel, 1964)
Producer: Howard Hawks
Associate Producer: Paul Helmick
Assistant Director: Tom Connors, Jr.
Screenplay: John Fenton Murray, Steve McNeil (and, uncredited, Leigh Brackett?), based on the story "The Girl Who Almost Got Away," by Pat Frank
Cinematographer: Russell Harlan
Art Directors: Alexander Golitzen, Tambi Larsen
Music: Henry Mancini
Makeup: Bud Westmore
Editor: Stuart Gilmore
Special Effects: Ben McMahon
Cast: Rock Hudson (Roger Willoughby), Paula Prentiss (Abigail Page), Maria Perschy (Isolde "Easy" Mueller), John McGiver (William Cadwalader), Charlene Holt (Tex Connors), Roscoe Karns (Major Phipps), Norman Alden (John Screaming Eagle), Forrest Lewis (Skaggs), Regis Toomey (Bagley)
Running Time: 120 minutes
Premier: January 29, 1964
16 mm. Rental: Universal 16

RED LINE 7000 (Paramount/Laurel, 1965)
Producer: Howard Hawks
Second Unit Director: Bruce Kessler
Assistant Director: Dick Moder
Screenplay: Hawks, George Kirgo
Cinematographer: Milton Krasner
Art Directors: Hal Pereira, Arthur Lonergan
Music: Nelson Riddle
Songs: Hoagy Carmichael, Harold Adamson, and Carol Conners
Makeup: Wally Westmore
Editors: Stuart Gilmore, Bill Brame
Special Effects: Paul K. Lerpae
Cast: James Caan (Mike Marsh), Laura Devon (Julie Kazarian), Gail Hire (Holly MacGregor), Charlene Holt (Lindy Bonaparte), John Robert Crawford (Ned Arp), Marianna Hill (Gabrielle), James Ward (Dan McCall), Norman Alden (Pat Kazarian), George Takei (Kato)
Running Time: 110 minutes
Premier: November 10, 1965 (Charlotte, North Carolina)
16 mm. Rental: Films Inc., Paramount Non-Theatrical

EL DORADO (Paramount/Laurel, 1967)
Producer: Howard Hawks
Assistant Director: Andrew J. Durkus
Screenplay: Leigh Brackett, from the novel *The Stars in Their Courses,* by Harry Brown
Cinematographer: Harold Rosson
Art Directors: Hal Pereira, Carl Anderson
Music: Nelson Riddle
Makeup: Wally Westmore
Editor: John Woodcock
Special Photographic Effects: Paul K. Lerpae
Cast: John Wayne (Cole Thornton), Robert Mitchum (J. P. Harrah), James Caan (Alan Bourdillon Traherne/Mississippi), Charlene Holt (Maudie), Michele Carey (Joey MacDonald), Arthur Hunnicut (Bull Harris), Christopher George (Nelse McLeod), R. G. Armstrong (Kevin MacDonald), Edward Asner (Bart Jason), Paul Fix (Doc Miller), Robert Donner (Milt), Jim Davis (Jason's foreman), Johnny Crawford (Luke MacDonald), Olaf Wieghorst (Swedish gunsmith)
Running Time: 122 minutes
Premier: December 31, 1966 (Denver); released June 7, 1967
16 mm. Rental: Films Inc., Paramount Non-Theatrical

RIO LOBO (Cinema Center/Malabar, 1970)
Producer: Howard Hawks
Associate Producer: Paul Helmick
Assistant Director: Mike Moder
Second Unit Director: Yakima Canutt
Screenplay: Leigh Brackett and Burton Wohl
Story: Burton Wohl
Cinematographer: William Clothier
Art Director: William R. Kiernan
Production Design: Robert Smith
Sets: William Kiernan
Music: Jerry Goldsmith
Editor: John Woodcock
Special Effects: A. D. Flowers, Clifford P. Wenger
Cast: John Wayne (Cord McNally), Jorge Rivero (Pierre Cordona), Chris
Mitchum (Tuscarora), Jack Elam (Phillips), Jennifer O'Neill (Shasta), Susana
Dosamantes (Maria), Sherry Lansing (Amelita), Victor French (Ketcham),
David Huddleston (Dr. Jones), Mike Henry (Sheriff Hendricks), Bill
Williams (Sheriff Cronin), Jim Davis (Riley), Robert Conner (Whitey),
George Plimpton, Edward Faulkner, Hank Worden
Running Time: 114 minutes
Premier: November 6, 1970 (Chicago); released December 16
16 mm. Rental: Audio Brandon Films, Swank

Index